PNSO Encyclopedia for Children

THE SECRETS OF ANCIENT SEA MONSTERS

PNSO Encyclopedia for Children
THE SECRETS OF ANCIENT SEA MONSTERS

Illustrations: ZHAO Chuang / Text: YANG Yang

A PNSO Production

BROWN BOOKS KIDS

© 2015, PNSO

All rights reserved. English language rights arranged through Media Solutions Japan (info@mediasolutions.jp) in conjunction with CA-Link International LLC. No part of this book may be used or reproduced in any manner without written permission except in the case of brief quotations embodied in critical articles or reviews.

PNSO Encyclopedia for Children: subtitle by Yang Yang and Zhao Chuang

The Secrets of Ancient Sea Monsters

Brown Books Kids
16250 Knoll Trail Drive, Suite 205
Dallas / New York
www.BrownBooksKids.com
(972) 381-0009

A New Era in Publishing®

Publisher's Cataloging-In-Publication Data

Names: Yang, Yang (Writer of children's encyclopedia), author. | Zhao, Chuang, illustrator. | Chen, Mo, translator. | PNSO (Organization), production company.
Title: The secrets of ancient sea monsters / illustrations: ZHAO Chuang ; text: YANG Yang ; [translator, Chen Mo].
Description: Dallas ; New York : Brown Books Kids, [2021] | Series: PNSO encyclopedia for children; [3] | Translated from the Chinese published in 2015. | "A PNSO production." | Interest age level: 010-012. | Includes bibliographical references and index. | Summary: "Learn about the sea creatures who lurked beneath the ripples and waves while dinosaurs walked and pterosaurs soared above!"--Provided by publisher.
Identifiers: ISBN 9781612545196
Subjects: LCSH: Marine animals, Fossil--Encyclopedias, Juvenile. | Prehistoric animals--Encyclopedias, Juvenile. | CYAC: Marine animals, Fossil--Encyclopedias. | Prehistoric animals--Encyclopedias.
Classification: LCC QE842 .Y36 2021 | DDC 567.903--dc23

ISBN 978-1-61254-519-6
LCCN 2021900890

Printed in China
10 9 8 7 6 5 4 3 2 1

For more information or to contact the author, please go to www.BrownBooks.com.

This book is dedicated to:

Napoléon Bonaparte, member of the Institut de France.
We thank him for his contributions to paleontology
research, especially with regards to the Mosasaurs.
We believe that the mission of education is to pass on
kindness and happiness to the next generation.

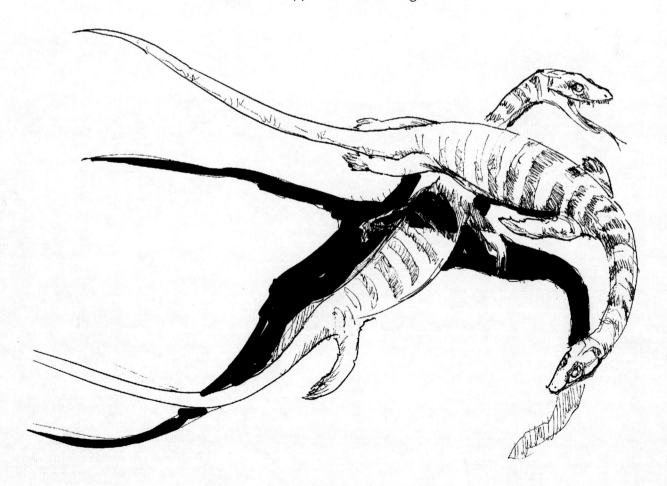

Contents List

xii	Foreword
xiii	Author's Preface
2	Notes for Reading
4	Scary Prehistoric Aquatic Reptiles
6	Precious Fossils
8	Main Content
164	Index
166	Reference
170	About the Authors

Fossil Index

vii	*Prognathodon* fossil
xi	Plesiosaur fossil
1	Mosasaur fossil
8	*Elasmosaurus* fossil
10	*Yuzhoupliosaurus* fossil
78	*Peipehsuchus* fossil
80	*Sarcosuchus* fossil
102	Mosasaur fossil
104	*Mosasaurus* upper jaw fossil
130	*Temnodontosaurus* fossil
132	*Ichthyosaurus* fossil

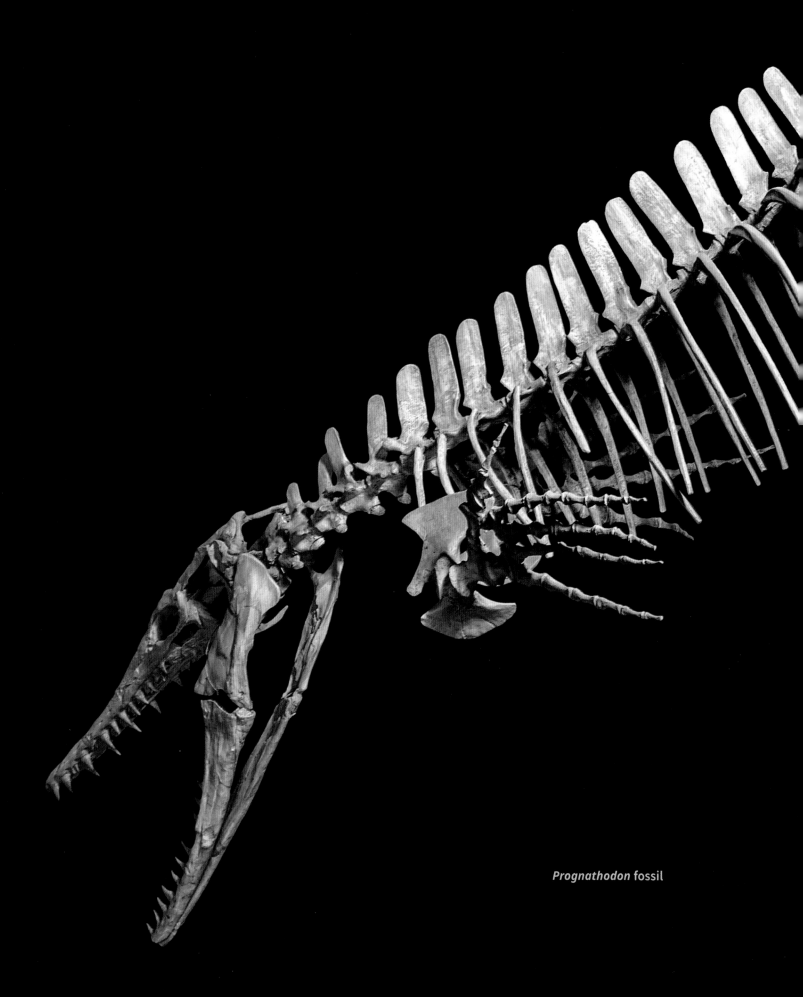

Prognathodon fossil

Table of Contents

8 Origins of Syngnathiformes Order and Sauropterygian Fossils
10 Period of Existence of Syngnathiformes Order and Sauropterygians in the Mesozoic Era

Syngnathiformes Order

- **12** An excellent swimmer in the deep sea: *Askeptosaurus*
- **14** Keeping a low profile: *Anshunsaurus*

Sauropterygian

Placodontia Order

- **16** Like a giant sea turtle: *Placochelys*
- **18** Bad at swimming: *Sinocyamodus*
- **20** Growing shells: *Placodus*
- **22** Barnacles, I'm coming!: *Psephoderma*
- **24** Where is my lunch?: *Psephochelys*

Eosauropterygia Suborder

- **26** Catching fish: *Nothosaurus*
- **28** *Nothosaurus giganteus*: The largest *Nothosaurus*
- **30** *Lariosaurus*: Fierce hunter in the shallow sea
- **32** Living in the Triassic sea in present-day Guizhou: *Lariosaurus xingyiensis*
- **34** A *Ceresiosaurus* preying on a *Pachypleurosaurus*
- **36** A *Pistosaurus* hunting a squid
- **38** *Yunguisaurus*: Trying to adapt to living in the water
- **40** *Eretmosaurus*: An excellent rower
- **42** The *Muraenosaurus* looks like a walrus
- **44** *Trinacromerum*: Its thighbones have three pointy ends
- **46** *Cimoliasaurus*: It has almost no relatives!
- **48** A *Rhomaleosaurus* with a keen nose
- **50** *Plesiosaurus*: A long neck and a short tail
- **52** A *Cryptoclidus* with horrifying teeth
- **54** A *Kronosaurus* preying on a *Woolungasaurus*

78 **Origins of Archosauria Fossils**

80 **Period of Existence of Archosauria Fossils in the Mesozoic Era**

Protorothyrididae Family

56 *Kaiwhekea*: Able to see 3D images

58 The clever *Elasmosaurus*

60 A *Styxosaurus* getting noticed by a *Tylosaurus*

62 *Bishanopliosaurus*: Living in fresh water

64 *Peloneustes*: The little cutie in the *Pliosauridae* family

66 *Kronosaurus*: The terrifying marine dominator

68 *Brachauchenius*: A witness of the extinction of the Plesiosaurs

70 A *Polycotylus* hunts for ammonites

72 A *Liopleurodon* hunts a *Eustreptospondylus*

74 Preferring fresh water: *Yuzhoupliosaurus*

76 *Macroplata*: The sprinting champion in the sea

82 *Tanystropheus*: It has a super long neck!

84 *Dinocephalosaurus*: A "vacuum cleaner" in water

Crocodylomorpha Superorder

86 *Dakosaurus*: A large, fierce-looking mouth

88 A *Sarcosuchus* attacks a *Suchomimus*

90 A fast runner: *Junggarsuchus*

92 The *Armadillosuchus* that lives on land

94 *Metriorhynchus*: A defenseless sea crocodile

96 The *Peipehsuchus* that loves eating fish

Choristodera Order

98 *Hyphalosaurus*: Living in the lakes

100 *Monjurosuchus*: A common creature in Liaoxi, China

Table of Contents

102 Origins of Squamata Fossils

104 Period of Existence of Squamata Fossils in the Mesozoic Era

Mosasauroidea Superfamily

106 | *Aigialosaurus*: The ancestor of the *Mosasaurus*!

108 | *Angolasaurus*: Founder of Mosasaurs

110 | *Dallasaurus*: The smallest Mosasaur

112 | *Plioplatecarpus*: It can swallow prey wider than its head!

114 | A pregnant *Plioplatecarpus*

116 | *Clidastes*: What a great swimmer!

118 | *Selmasaurus*: It can't get its mouth to open any wider

120 | *Hainosaurus*: A huge appetite

122 | *Plotosaurus*: The most advanced marine reptile

124 | A *Mosasaurus* hunting an *Archelon*

126 | A *Tylosaurus* preying on a small *Mosasaurus*

128 | The *Globidens* with unusual teeth

130 Origins of Ichthyopterygia Fossils

132 Period of Existence of Ichthyopterygia Fossils in the Mesozoic Era

Ichthyopterygia Superorder

134 | *Ichthyosaurus*: Revealing the mystery in the ocean

136 | Dancing in water: *Utatsusaurus*

138 | The large-eyed *Chaohusaurus*

140 | *Shastasaurus*: Is it the largest Ichthyosaurus?

142 | *Besanosaurus*: Spreading its offspring around the world

144 | *Californosaurus*: It has dorsal fins!

146 | *Cymbospondylus*: Master of the sea in the Triassic

148 | The *Mixosaurus* with its diamond-shaped tail fin

150 | A *Qianichthyosaurus* chases a small fish

152 | *Shonisaurus*: A "submarine" in the sea

154 | A *Stenopterygius* leaping out of the water

156 | *Excalibosaurus*: Mouth Shaped Like a Sword

158 | *Eurhinosaurus*: Samurai of the sea

160 | *Ophthalmosaurus*: It has huge eyes!

162 | A *Platypterygius* hunting an *Archelon*

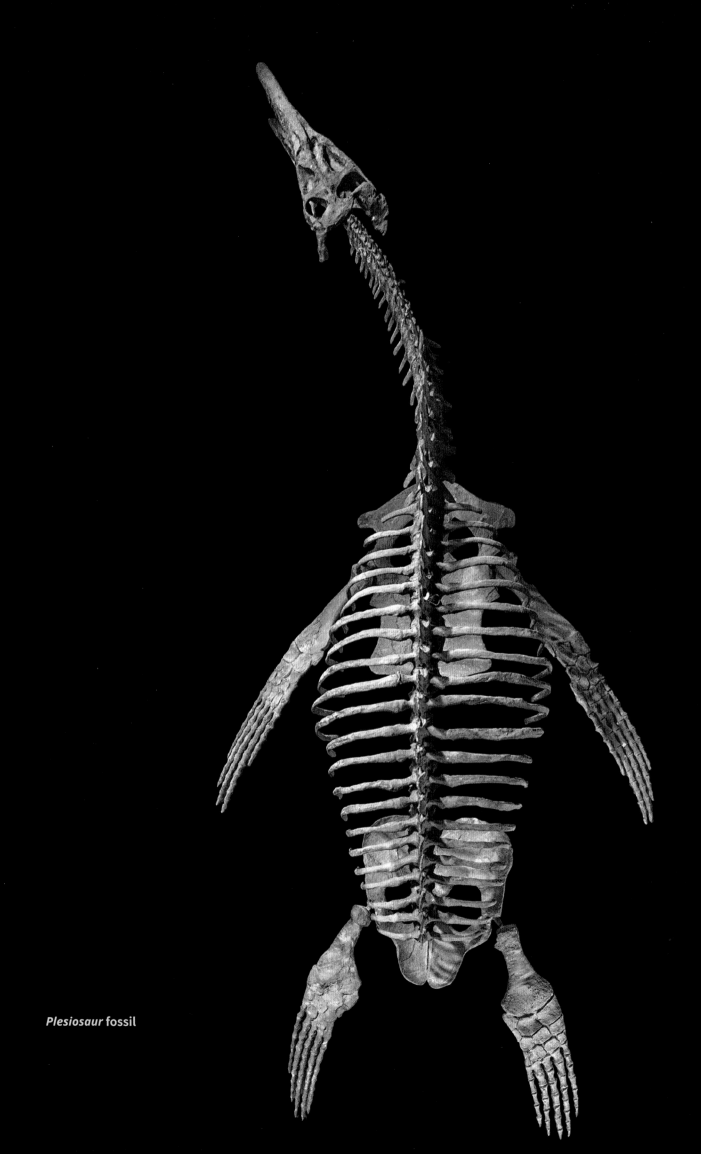

Plesiosaur fossil

Foreword

Paleontologist Curator and Chairman of the Division of Paleontology, AMNH Science Consultant for English Publications of PNSO Dr. Mark A. Norell's Introduction to the Works by ZHAO Chuang and YANG Yang

I am a paleontologist at one of the world's great museums. I get to spend my days surrounded by dinosaur bones. Whether it is in Mongolia excavating, in China studying, in New York analyzing data, or anywhere on the planet writing, teaching, or lecturing, dinosaurs are not only my interest, but my livelihood.

Most scientists, even the most brilliant ones, work in very closed societies. A system which, no matter how hard they try, is still unapproachable to average people. Maybe it's due to the complexities of mathematics, difficulties in understanding molecular biochemistry, or reconciling complex theory with actual data. No matter what, this behavior fosters boredom and disengagement. Personality comes in as well, and most scientists lack the communication skills necessary to make their efforts interesting and approachable. People are left being intimidated by science. But dinosaurs are special—people of all ages love them. So dinosaurs foster a great opportunity to teach science to everyone by tapping into something everyone is interested in.

That's why Yang Yang and Zhao Chuang are so important. Both are extraordinarily talented, very smart, but neither are scientists. Instead they use art and words as a medium to introduce dinosaur science to everyone from small children to grandparents—and even to scientists working in other fields!

Zhao Chuang's paintings, sculptures, drawings and films are state of the art representations of how these fantastic animals looked and behaved. They are drawn from the latest discoveries and his close collaboration with leading paleontologists. Yang Yang's writing is more than mere description. Instead she weaves stories through the narrative or makes the descriptions engaging and humorous. The subjects are so approachable that her stories can be read to small children, and young readers can discover these animals and explore science on their own. Through our fascination with dinosaurs, important concepts of geology, biology, and evolution are learned in a fun way. Zhao Chuang and Yang Yang are the world's best, and it is an honor to work with them.

Author's Preface

We are not alone in this world; we share it with others.
——A word to the fathers and mothers of our young readers

As I write this, I am sitting in the shade of my courtyard. Above in the trees, the cicadas are incessantly chirping, with their noises filling the air. Since the beginning of late spring, they have been happily chirping away every day. Happily? Well, I rarely see them; they are either hiding deep down in the dark soil biding their time until they reach maturity, or lying on the tree branches, enjoying a reclusive life. I know this without having to see them; as I listen to the sounds which tease my ear, I know that they are living a merry life in the world that we share with them.

At this moment, my daughter is chasing an ant that is moving on the ground; occasionally, she interrupts me with her giggles. She finds leaves which were blown off the trees by wind the night before and are now lying on the ground. Picking them up in bunches, she comes over to show me her new discovery. I tell her that these are leaves that have fallen from the trees. Soon after, she grabs a few rose petals, acting as if she is going to consume them. I quickly instruct her that these are flowers and that flowers cannot be eaten. Maybe she does not understand what I am saying; she has just learned to crawl, and she is still unable to talk. Because of this she probably does not recognize and identify the ants, leaves, and flowers, but nevertheless, she gets great enjoyment from watching them, just as she does from seeing me, as she giggles playfully. For her, there are very few differences between the ants, leaves, and flowers on the one hand, and her mom and dad, aunts and uncles on the other. She has great curiosity toward all these things which share this world with her.

I can't really identify at what point adults gradually begin to lose this magical sense of curiosity, or when we begin to overlook all of the other types of life and arrogantly consider humans as the most important subjects, simply because now we are the predominant group on this planet.

The irony is that if there is no other life, humans would no longer be able to support themselves and would perish. However, we often do not think in this way. We are accustomed to understanding life through such a paradigm: chicken is delicious food, from which you can make roast chicken or smoked chicken; the beef we get from cattle tastes good and has high nutritional value. We are often indoctrinated with such knowledge, so it is no surprise that this often inadvertently breeds our selfish arrogance.

I often find myself thinking about this problem, so for the longest time, I have desired to write an encyclopedia for children, one that introduces them to a wide variety of other types of life. This encyclopedic book should not be like ones written for adults; it is not merely a large number of details showing an animal's length, height, and weight. Its purpose is to be far more than a pile of data, to go beyond just a list of knowledge and facts; the essence of this work is meant to be like the chorus of afternoon cicadas. You cannot see them, yet you hear their voices, just like those ants which my daughter find enchanting—you forge a close connection with them despite not knowing their specifics. For children, everything in this world is incredibly fresh. They want to know: beyond themselves, their family, their kindergarten teachers, and fellow students, what else is out there in this world? In addition to their home, their kindergarten, and the city that they live in, how much further beyond does this world extend to? They want to move beyond the present and the past that they can remember to know how far the world will go. Their curiosity is a key which unlocks the entire world. All they ask us is to leave the door open. They can figure out the rest on their own.

Hence, our collection of stories within the PNSO Encyclopedia for Children is meant to impress our children with an understanding of the world beyond humans. Children should realize that this world is not only for us; others share it with us. The "others" may be other forms of life or something wonderful that exists in our human imagination. In short, these exist in our present world, whether in our day-to-day reality or the magical expanses of our imagination.

To be aware of their existence is more than a form of knowledge. It is a strength by which our inner world expands and broadens. If that happens, we will be less likely to become arrogant because of our ignorance, to begrudge over small things, or to hinder our long-term future because of immediate gains. We can avoid being selfish, narrow-minded, and fearful. We should respect all lives because they have accompanied us throughout our existence and are sharing this world with us. The world is so dauntingly big; it is vital that we work together in harmony with each other to move forward.

Often, the babbling of a young child constantly reminds me how important it is to keep alive the curiosity of childhood. It is that curiosity that allows us to walk humbly in this vast world. I hope that as you read this book with your children, you may nurture their sense of curiosity and accompany them in exploring this wondrous world.

杨杨
YANG Yang
August 1, 2015, in Beijing

Mosasaur fossil

Notes for Reading

❶ Period of Existence of Aquatic Reptiles
(for selected species)

❷ Scales: 50cm, 1m, 5m, 25m
Reference objects: basketball, father, mother, boy, girl, bus, plane
Diagrams showing prehistoric aquatic reptiles' sizes: prehistoric aquatic reptile's silhouette (when the size of the prehistoric aquatic reptile is less than 1 unit of the scale), prehistoric aquatic reptile's outlines, prehistoric aquatic reptile's draft sketches

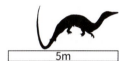

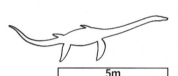

CMYK color codes for scales, reference objects, and diagrams showing prehistoric aquatic reptiles' sizes

Dark background: C0 M0 Y0 K80 ■
Light background: C0 M0 Y0 K20 ▪

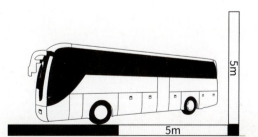

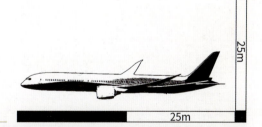

| ~145.0 | 100.5 | 66.0 |

Late Jurassic | Early Cretaceous | Late Cretaceous
Cretaceous
Mesozoic
Phanerozoic Eon

Scary Prehistoric Aquatic Reptiles

The sea is vast and mysterious, a delight for almost all people. We often swim in it or play on its shore. We enjoy the sea because seawater cools our body, making us feel wonderful. But another wonder, the mysterious inhabitants living deep down, remains hidden to us all.

Who are they? They are animals living in the sea, like the scary sharks, the cute dolphins, the slow-moving turtles, and a great variety

of fish. We have a chance to see these, but the ones that I am going to talk about are marine reptiles. Some of these could grow to more than twenty meters long. They include crocodiles that could both walk and swim; animals that were like turtles but were much fiercer; ones who could swallow the smaller dinosaurs in one bite . . . You probably feel puzzled: some of you have gone diving but never seen these. That's because these creatures lived hundreds of millions of years ago, and an extinction event about 66 million years ago wiped out the most of them. They were called prehistoric aquatic reptiles. Some of them lived not in the ocean but in freshwater. They were the most powerful water-borne rulers that ever lived as they were both numerous and large. In a relatively short period, they grew from small guys who fed on small fish and shrimp to huge, terrifying killers, unrivaled by anyone.

Precious Fossils

Although prehistoric aquatic reptiles have become extinct, we still know a lot about them, thanks to their precious fossils.

Fossils of prehistoric aquatic reptiles are rare because most of them lived in water all the time. When they died, their bones quickly decomposed without a trace. By chance, some of the bones would be quickly buried by sand and mud and eventually formed fossils. But those fossils were likely to be buried underwater for a long time, with no one knowing about them.

Therefore, it was geological changes that allowed scientists to discover prehistoric aquatic reptile fossils. These shifted the aquatic environment, where these reptiles lived, to land pieces with their fossils buried underground.

Thanks to these fossils, we can rebuild their images and reconstruct the world in which they lived. Now, let us board this "book submarine" and go deep into the water to see the true face of these monsters!

Origins of Syngnathiformes Order and Sauropterygian Fossils

Compiled by: PNSO

14	*Anshunsaurus* — Fossil Origin: China, Asia		12	*Askeptosaurus* — Fossil Origin: Italy and Switzerland, Europe
18	*Sinocyamodus* — Fossil Origin: China, Asia		16	*Placochelys* — Fossil Origin: Germany, Europe
24	*Psephochelys* — Fossil Origin: China, Asia		20	*Placodus* — Fossil Origin: Europe and Asia
32	*Lariosaurus xingyiensis* — Fossil Origin: China, Asia		22	*Psephoderma* — Fossil Origin: Europe
38	*Yunguisaurus* — Fossil Origin: China, Asia		26	*Nothosaurus* — Fossil Origin: Europe and Asia
62	*Bishanopliosaurus* — Fossil Origin: China, Asia		28	*Nothosaurus giganteus* — Fossil Origin: Germany, Europe
74	*Yuzhoupliosaurus* — Fossil Origin: China, Asia		30	*Lariosaurus* — Fossil Origin: Europe and Asia
			34	*Ceresiosaurus* — Fossil Origin: Switzerland, Europe
44	*Trinacromerum* — Fossil Origin: United States, North America		36	*Pistosaurus* — Fossil Origin: Germany and France, Europe
46	*Cimoliasaurus* — Fossil Origin: North America, Europe, and Oceania		40	*Eretmosaurus* — Fossil Origin: United Kingdom, Europe
58	*Elasmosaurus* — Fossil Origin: United States, North America		42	*Muraenosaurus* — Fossil Origin: United Kingdom and France, Europe
60	*Styxosaurus* — Fossil Origin: United States, North America		48	*Rhomaleosaurus* — Fossil Origin: United Kingdom, Europe
68	*Brachauchenius* — Fossil Origin: North America and South America		50	*Plesiosaur* — Fossil Origin: United Kingdom and Germany, Europe
70	*Polycotylus* — Fossil Origin: North America and Europe		52	*Cryptoclidus* — Fossil Origin: Europe and South America
			64	*Peloneustes* — Fossil Origin: United Kingdom, Europe
			72	*Liopleurodon* — Fossil Origin: France, United Kingdom, and Russia, Europe
			76	*Macroplata* — Fossil Origin: Europe

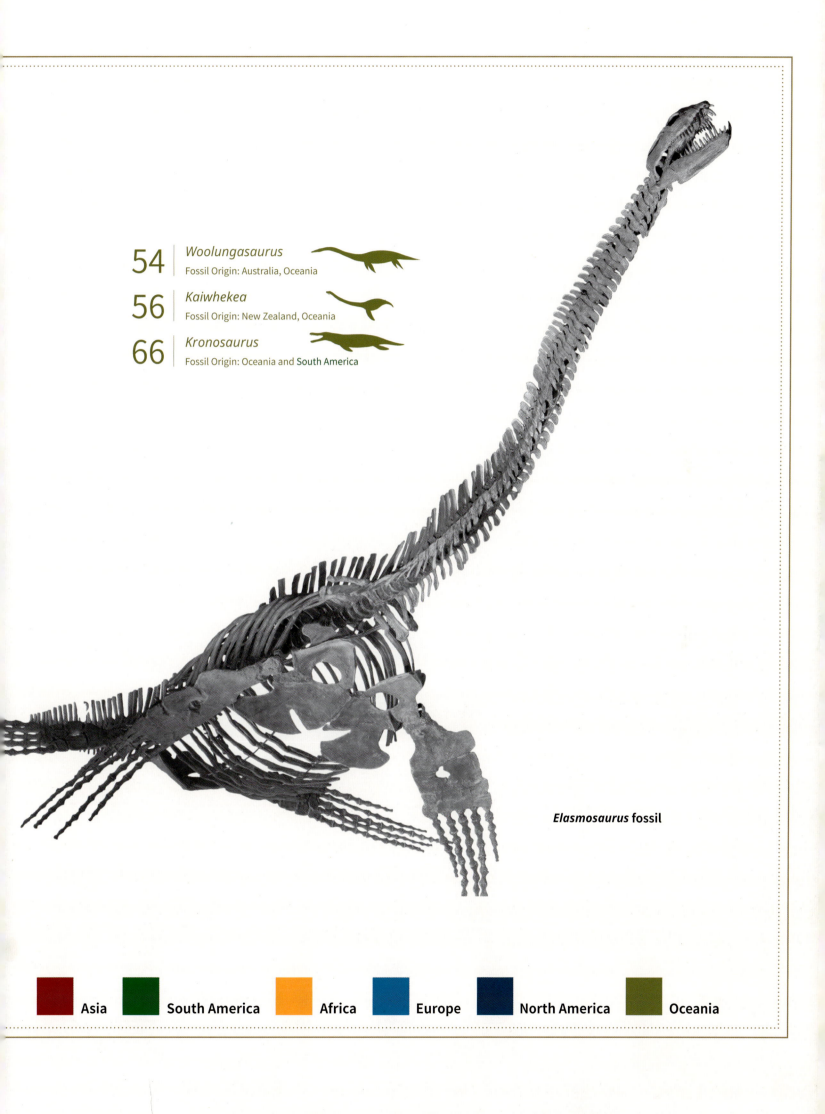

54	*Woolungasaurus* Fossil Origin: Australia, Oceania
56	*Kaiwhekea* Fossil Origin: New Zealand, Oceania
66	*Kronosaurus* Fossil Origin: Oceania and South America

Elasmosaurus fossil

Asia | South America | Africa | Europe | North America | Oceania

Period of Existence of Syngnathiformes Order and Sauropterygians in the Mesozoic Era

Compiled by: PNSO

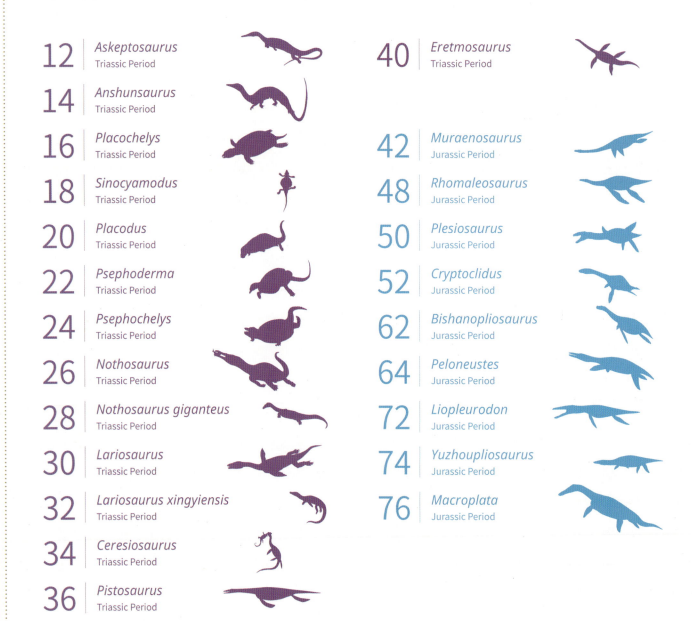

Yuzhoupliosaurus fossil

44	*Trinacromerum* Cretaceous Period
46	*Cimoliasaurus* Cretaceous Period
54	*Woolungasaurus* Cretaceous Period
56	*Kaiwhekea* Cretaceous Period
58	*Elasmosaurus* Cretaceous Period
60	*Styxosaurus* Cretaceous Period
66	*Kronosaurus* Cretaceous Period
68	*Brachauchenius* Cretaceous Period
70	*Polycotylus* Cretaceous Period

An excellent swimmer in the deep sea
Askeptosaurus

The *Askeptosaurus* has adapted well to life in the sea; it has a long and thin body, rather like an eel, and it is good at swimming. Its eyes are large and round with excellent eyesight, which allows it to move around freely in the deep sea. It has a ring of bones that surrounds its eyes so that the enormous hydraulic pressure of the deep sea will not crush its eyeballs. Despite having these features to adapt to living in the deep sea, the *Askeptosaurus* sometimes comes on land, especially when it is time to lay its eggs.

Askeptosaurus

Body size: Approximately 2 meters
Diet: Fish
Period of existence: Triassic
Fossil origin: Italy and Switzerland, Europe

SYNGNATHIFORMES ORDER | 15

Keeping a low profile
Anshunsaurus

An *Anshunsaurus* steps over a tree trunk that has fallen into the water while enjoying the view. Such is its pleasant life.

The *Anshunsaurus* likes to keep a low profile; even though it is capable of conquering, it prefers to share the beautiful sea world with the members of the *Ichthyosauridae* family.

The *Anshunsaurus* has a slender body and a long paddle-like tail, which can propel the *Anshunsaurus* forward with great power.

Anshunsaurus

Body size: Approximately 3.5 meters
Diet: Fish
Period of existence: Triassic
Fossil origin: China, Asia

Like a giant sea turtle
Placochelys

If nobody tells you that this is an ancient creature, you will probably think that this is a big turtle, because it looks like one.

This creature is called *Placochelys*. The carapace on its back looks like a broad shield, with nail-like knobs dotted on top of it. The *Placochelys*'s snout is tough, almost toothless, making it quite like a bird's beak. It can use this beak to peck at shelled shellfish, shrimp, and crabs. Its flippers look quite like those of a turtle, with the obvious difference being that it has toes at the end of its flippers.

Placochelys

Body size: Approximately 0.9 meters
Diet: Shrimp and crabs
Period of existence: Triassic
Fossil origin: Germany, Europe

SAUROPTERYGIAN PLACODONTIA ORDER | 17

Bad at swimming
Sinocyamodus

The *Sinocyamodus* is unlike other members in its *Cyamodontoidea* family. Its carapace is in one piece, not composed of two halves. Furthermore, other members have their forelimbs fully covered in scales, but the *Sinocyamodus*'s limbs are bare. The *Sinocyamodus* is small, with an exceptionally long tail, and no scales or plates on its abdomen. It is terrible at swimming, so it has to live in shallow waters, preying on crustaceans close to the river bank.

SAUROPTERYGIAN PLACODONTIA ORDER | 19

Sinocyamodus

Body size: 0.5 meters (juveniles)
Diet: Shellfish
Period of existence: Triassic
Fossil origin: China, Asia

SAUROPTERYGIAN PLACODONTIA ORDER | 21

Growing shells
Placodus

Even though the *Placodus* lives in water, it has yet to develop the more advanced flippers but relies on its webs and its flat tail to move around. An unusual feature is its stiff and rigid armor, which was useful for the slow-moving *Placodus*. Thanks to the armor, it does not have to fear attacks from those fast and ruthless predators.

Placodus

Body size: Approximately 2 meters
Diet: Mollusks, brachiopods, and shellfish
Period of existence: Triassic
Fossil origin: Europe and Asia

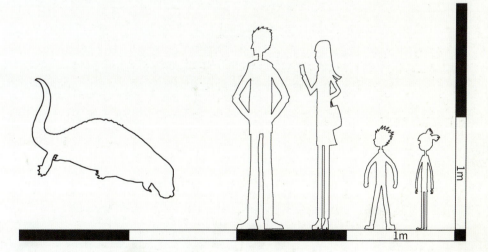

Barnacles, I'm coming!
Psephoderma

The *Psephoderma* is enormous. It can grow up to nearly two meters, but it is not good at swimming. It practices swimming every day in order to get better and adapt to life in the sea! Now, pushing itself forward with its wide feet, it is half-swimming, half-crawling, and trying to catch its favorite food—barnacles!

Psephoderma

Body size: Approximately 1.8 meters
Diet: Mollusks
Period of existence: Triassic
Fossil origin: Europe

Where is my lunch?
Psephochelys

It's lunchtime, but the *Psephochelys*'s lunch hasn't arrived yet. It is half-swimming, half-walking around in the water with its mouth wide open, looking for something to eat. It would love to be able to speed through the water, like some of the other creatures. It wishes it could hunt better and worry less about starving, but it is not a good swimmer. Nevertheless, *Psephochelys* has strength. The slow-moving creature doesn't have to worry about being attacked by predators because its back and its abdomen are protected by armored plates and rib-like gastralia.

Psephochelys

Body size: Approximately 0.6 meters
Diet: Shellfish
Period of existence: Triassic
Fossil origin: China, Asia

SAUROPTERYGIAN EOSAUROPTERYGIA SUBORDER | 27

Catching fish
Nothosaurus

The *Nothosaurus* was one of the first reptiles to dwell in the ocean. It spends most of its time in the sea, catching fish, smaller reptiles, and cephalopods. The *Nothosaurus* only occasionally comes up to the surface and on land For example, during the mating season, it comes onto the beach to lay eggs.

The *Nothosaurus*'s fingers (and toes) are webbed. It propels forward in water by paddling with its tail and four webbed limbs.

Nothosaurus

Body size: 4–6 meters
Diet: Fish
Period of existence: Triassic
Fossil origin: Europe and Asia

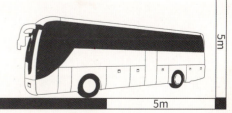

Nothosaurus giganteus
The largest *Nothosaurus*

The *Nothosaurus giganteus* is called "*giganteus*" because of its enormous size, being the largest member of the *Nothosauridae* family, with a body length of up to six meters.

The fossil of *Nothosaurus giganteus* was discovered in Germany. So far, only a few fossils of the *Nothosaurus giganteus* have been discovered, and these are fragmented and incomplete.

SAUROPTERYGIAN EOSAUROPTERYGIA SUBORDER | 29

Nothosaurus giganteus

Body size: Approximately 6 meters
Diet: Fish
Period of existence: Triassic
Fossil origin: Germany, Europe

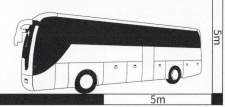

Lariosaurus
Fierce hunter in the shallow sea

The *Lariosaurus* is the smallest member of the *Nothosauria* family, with a body length of sixty centimeters. It is a strange-looking creature. Its forelimbs are more advanced than those of its relatives, with not only flippers but also five toes on each of its hind limbs. The incomplete evolution makes it a mediocre swimmer. It spends most of its time on dry land or occasionally hunting in shallow waters. Its teeth suggest that it is a fierce hunter.

SAUROPTERYGIAN EOSAUROPTERYGIA SUBORDER | 31

Lariosaurus

Body size: 0.6–2 meters
Diet: Fish
Period of existence: Triassic
Fossil origin: Europe and Asia

Living in the Triassic sea in present-day Guizhou
Lariosaurus xingyiensis

The fossil of *Lariosaurus xingyiensis*, the first member of the *Lariosaurus* family to be discovered in China, was found in Xingyi City, Guizhou Province.

The *Lariosaurus xingyiensis* looks like a lizard; its neck is long, flexible, and can swing easily in water.

The *Lariosaurus xingyiensis* had a slender head, and its mouth is full of sharp teeth, which can pierce the bodies of fish and mollusks.

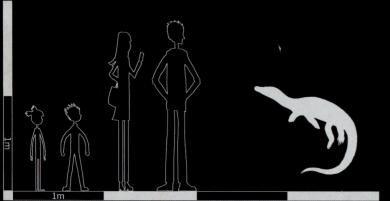

Lariosaurus xingyiensis

Body size: Approximately 2 meters
Diet: Fish
Period of existence: Triassic
Fossil origin: China, Asia

SAUROPTERYGIAN EOSAUROPTERYGIA SUBORDER | **33**

A *Ceresiosaurus*
preying on a *Pachypleurosaurus*

A small *Pachypleurosaurus* is all grown up, ready to leave its mother and hunt on its own. It swims around happily in the water, and soon it notices a group of defenseless fish. The small *Pachypleurosaurus* is delighted; it opens its mouth, ready to swallow them up. Suddenly, an enormous *Ceresiosaurus* jumps out from behind and mercilessly bites into the neck of the *Pachypleurosaurus*. No matter how the *Pachypleurosaurus* struggles, the *Ceresiosaurus* doesn't let go. The little *Pachypleurosaurus* cries out in fear!

The small *Pachypleurosaurus* isn't aware that the attacker, a member of the *Nothosauridae* family, is an excellent swimmer. With its sleek body and flippers, it can attack with great speed, striking its prey when they least expect it.

Ceresiosaurus
Body size: Approximately 4 meters
Diet: Fish
Period of existence: Triassic
Fossil origin: Switzerland, Europe

A *Pistosaurus*
hunting a squid

A *Pistosaurus* is getting ready to attack a resting squid. The squid is large, so the *Pistosaurus* chooses not to attack its prey head-on. Instead, it does it stealthily.

Just as the *Pistosaurus* is sneaking up close to the squid and about to attack, thinking that the victim will not notice, the squid suddenly wraps itself tightly around the *Pistosaurus*. The terrified *Pistosaurus* struggles to free itself from the squid's tentacles. The battle lasts for a long time until, eventually, the *Pistosaurus* subdues the giant squid.

Pistosaurus

Body size: Approximately 3 meters
Diet: Fish and squid
Period of existence: Triassic
Fossil origin: Germany and France, Europe

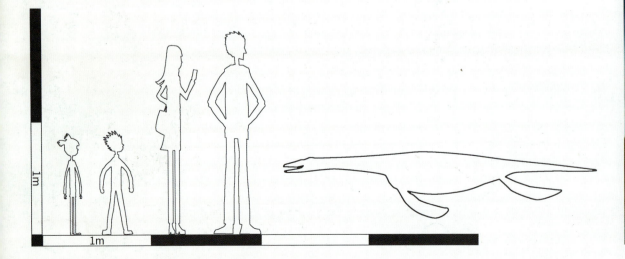

SAUROPTERYGIAN EOSAUROPTERYGIA SUBORDER | 37

Yunguisaurus
Trying to adapt to living in the water

The *Nothosauridae* family members did not live long before they disappeared from the water world, with their place taken by the *Plesiosauridae* family. This was a group that adapted extremely well to living in water, and they flourished for a long period of time until the end of the Cretaceous period, when the great extinction struck.

The *Yunguisaurus* was from the *Pistosauroidea* family, an intermediate link in evolution between the *Nothosauridae* and the *Plesiosauridae* families. It had a long tail that looked like the *Nothosaurus*'s. However, its limbs were much more advanced, like those found within the *Plesiosauridae* family.

SAUROPTERYGIAN EOSAUROPTERYGIA SUBORDER | 39

Yunguisaurus

Body size: Approximately 2 meters
Diet: Fish
Period of existence: Triassic
Fossil origin: China, Asia

Eretmosaurus
An excellent rower

The *Eretmosaurus* is one of the earliest members of the *Plesiosauridae* family. It has a long, slender body and four flippers. When scientists discovered it, they noticed that its flippers looked remarkably like paddles. They concluded that it most likely used them in the same way we use a paddle to move a raft forward. The root "eretmo" means "to row."

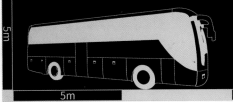

Eretmosaurus

Body size: 4–5 meters
Diet: Fish
Period of existence: Triassic
Fossil origin: United Kingdom, Europe

The *Muraenosaurus*
looks like a walrus

SAUROPTERYGIAN EOSAUROPTERYGIA SUBORDER | 43

The *Muraenosaurus* looks like a modern-day walrus, which is not surprising because it, too, is semi-aquatic. It can both swim around comfortably in water and climb onto the shore to walk around. It has a lot of room to move around.

The *Muraenosaurus* has an interesting way of hunting; it often exposes its head above the surface of the sea, floating around close to the seashore almost aimlessly. Its eyes, however, will constantly be fixed on the surface of the water. As soon as the *Muraenosaurus* notices any prey, it will charge and attack, ruthlessly biting into its victim.

Muraenosaurus

Body size: Approximately 6 meters
Diet: Fish and cephalopods
Period of existence: Jurassic
Fossil origin: United Kingdom and France, Europe

Trinacromerum
Its thighbones have three pointy ends

The fossil of the *Trinacromerum* was discovered in Kansas, in the United States. The roughly three-meter-long *Trinacromerum* has four flippers, which allow it to swim quickly. It loves to eat fish, and one gobbling of its big mouth often catches a large group of fish—those blind enough to swim past it.

Because its femur (thigh bone) has three sharp points, scientists have given it the name *Trinacromerum*, with "acro" meaning "tip" and "merum" meaning "thigh."

SAUROPTERYGIAN EOSAUROPTERYGIA SUBORDER

Trinacromerum

Body size: Approximately 3 meters
Diet: Small fish
Period of existence: Cretaceous
Fossil origin: United States, North America

Cimoliasaurus
It has almost no relatives!

The *Cimoliasaurus* is a large fellow, with a body that can reach thirteen to twenty-five meters. Its neck is long, and it has a pair of large eyes that gives it good eyesight to spot prey. The *Cimoliasaurus* belongs to a branch of the Plesiosauria order, the *Cimoliasauridae* family, a small group with few relatives.

Cimoliasaurus

Body size: 13–25 meters
Diet: Carnivorous
Period of existence: Cretaceous
Fossil origin: North America, Europe, and Oceania

25m

A *Rhomaleosaurus* with a keen nose

The *Rhomaleosaurus* has a large head and a rather short neck. These are not its most noteworthy features, however, because its nose deserves special mention. Its nose can trace the currents to smell other animals around it and figure out where to find its favorite foods, dead animals, friends, and enemies. Because of its splendid nose, it can easily hunt for prey whilst avoiding danger.

Rhomaleosaurus

Body size: Approximately 7 meters
Diet: Fish
Period of existence: Jurassic
Fossil origin: United Kingdom, Europe

Millions of Years Ago	252.17 ±0.06	~247.2	~237	201.3 ±0.2	174.1 ±1.0	163.5 ±1.0
Epoch	Early Triassic	Middle Triassic	Late Triassic		Early Jurassic	Middle Jurassic
Period		Triassic			Jurassic	
Era						
Eon						

SAUROPTERYGIAN EOSAUROPTERYGIA SUBORDER | 49

~145.0		100.5		66.0
Late Jurassic	Early Cretaceous		Late Cretaceous	
		Cretaceous		
Mesozoic				
Phanerozoic Eon				

Plesiosaurus

Body size: 3–5 meters
Diet: Fish and shellfish
Period of existence: Jurassic
Fossil origin: United Kingdom and Germany, Europe

Millions of Years Ago	252.17 ±0.06	~247.2	~237		201.3 ±0.2		174.1 ±1.0	163. ±1.
Epoch	Early Triassic	Middle Triassic	Late Triassic			Early Jurassic	Middle Jurassic	
Period			Triassic			Jurassic		
Era								
Eon								

SAUROPTERYGIAN EOSAUROPTERYGIA SUBORDER | 51

Plesiosaurus
A long neck and a short tail

The *Plesiosaurus* is the most famous member of the *Plesiosauridae* family; however, it is not as good at swimming as one may expect. Its neck is long but inflexible in bending. Its tail is short and can flap up and down to aid swimming. It has strong flippers, which could provide enough power to propel itself.

SAUROPTERYGIAN EOSAUROPTERYGIA SUBORDER | 53

A *Cryptoclidus*
with horrifying teeth

The *Cryptoclidus* is not a nice fellow to deal with. It has a mouth full of nearly one hundred scary-looking teeth. Even as it closes its mouth, some of its teeth still jut out, with the upper and lower rows crisscrossing. It must be a terrifying sight!

Cryptoclidus

Body size: Approximately 8 meters
Diet: Fish and mollusks
Period of existence: Jurassic
Fossil origin: Europe and South America

A *Kronosaurus* preying on a *Woolungasaurus*

A *Woolungasaurus* is hunting in the water. Before it has a chance to catch anything, it finds itself under attack from a *Kronosaurus*. Although the two creatures' sizes are similar, the *Kronosaurus* is clearly stronger. With little effort, it bites into the slender neck and small head of the *Woolungasaurus*. The *Woolungasaurus* tries to resist, but every struggle only moves the sharp teeth of the *Kronosaurus* deeper into the flesh.

Woolungasaurus

Body size: Approximately 9.5 meters
Diet: Fish
Period of existence: Cretaceous
Fossil origin: Oceania and South America

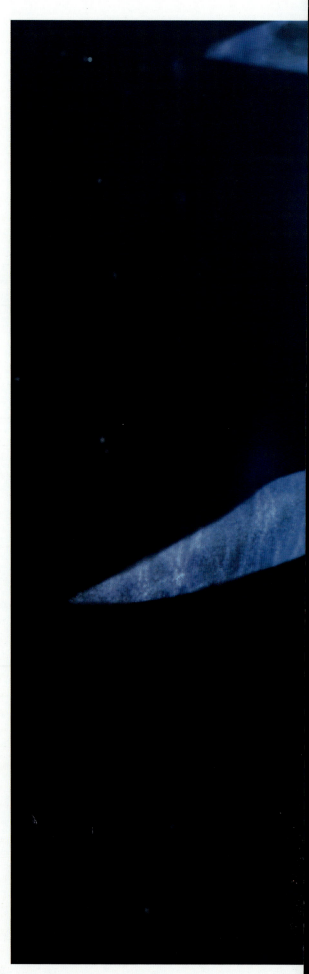

Kaiwhekea
Able to see 3D images

The *Kaiwhekea* has a skill that most of the other animals don't have: like humans, it can see in three dimensions. Because of this, the *Kaiwhekea* spends most of its time in the deep ocean where there is less light. Its keen vision gives it a greater advantage there, so it can easily prey on nearby creatures.

SAUROPTERYGIAN EOSAUROPTERYGIA SUBORDER | 57

The *Kaiwhekea* has about 170 small and narrow teeth. Because of this, the *Kaiwhekea* is not well-suited to attacking large prey. Instead, it eats small fish and mollusks.

Look at the unfortunate little fellow in its mouth. It is about to be greedily devoured by the *Kaiwhekea*!

Kaiwhekea

Body size: Approximately 7 meters
Diet: Small fish and mollusks
Period of existence: Cretaceous
Fossil origin: New Zealand, Oceania

The clever *Elasmosaurus*

The *Elasmosaurus* has a very small head, which makes biting larger prey difficult. To overcome that handicap, it has developed a clever way to hunt. The *Elasmosaurus* will hide quietly in the shallow water close to the shore, lifting its long neck and exposing its head above the surface.

SAUROPTERYGIAN EOSAUROPTERYGIA SUBORDER | 59

The small head is unlikely to be detected by any nearby prey, but the *Elasmosaurus*, with its keen vision, can quickly spot its target. Having gained the element of surprise as soon, it quickly lowers its head into the water and firmly holds down its prey.

Elasmosaurus

Body size: Approximately 14 meters
Diet: Fish
Period of existence: Cretaceous
Fossil origin: United States, North America

A *Styxosaurus* getting noticed by a *Tylosaurus*

The *Styxosaurus* never thought that it could find itself in such a fix; it is more than eleven meters long and is seldom bullied by others. But it is now in trouble, as a fifteen-meter *Tylosaurus* has made it a target. They have been fighting back and forth for a while, with the *Styxosaurus* out of breath after dodging the *Tylosaurus*'s attacks. Although the *Styxosaurus* has been fortunate enough to evade the *Tylosaurus*'s fifty razor-sharp teeth, it is not sure about being so lucky the next second!

The *Styxosaurus* belongs to the *Elasmosauridae*, a branch of the *Plesiosauridae* family. The neck of the *Styxosaurus* is long—almost the same length as the rest of the body. When scientists came across a specimen of the *Styxosaurus*, they discovered that the abdominal cavity of the *Styxosaurus* contained a hard, solid mass of stone. Some herbivorous dinosaurs have stones in their stomach to aid digestion, but for *Styxosaurus*, the stones are there to increase weight, so they submerge more easily.

Styxosaurus

Body size: 11–12 meters
Diet: Carnivorous
Period of existence: Cretaceous
Fossil origin: United States, North America

Bishanopliosaurus
Living in fresh water

The *Bishanopliosaurus* is a small-headed Plesiosaur with a body length of approximately four meters and a long neck.

Almost all Plesiosaurs live in the sea, but the *Bishanopliosaurus* is different; it lives in freshwater in the present-day Sichuan Basin. Because of this, scientists believe it is likely that the Sichuan Basin was once connected to the sea so that the *Bishanopliosaurus* could follow the flow of seawater into the Sichuan Basin.

Bishanopliosaurus

Body size: Approximately 4 meters
Diet: Fish
Period of existence: Jurassic
Fossil origin: China, Asia

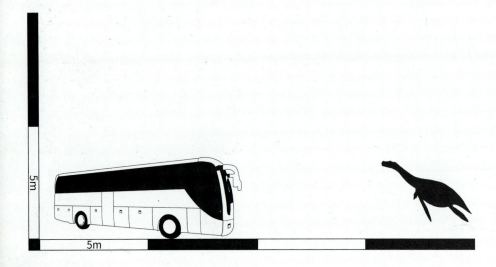

Peloneustes
The little cutie in the *Pliosauridae* family

The *Peloneustes* belongs to the *Pliosauridae* family, a branch of the Plesiosauria order. It is only three meters long, one of the smallest Pliosaurs. Unlike many of the other long-necked members of the *Plesiosauridae* family, all Pliosaurs have short necks.

The small *Peloneustes* is an exceptional swimmer. If you look carefully, you find that its hind fins are much larger than its front fins, which shows that it could move quickly in water. The *Peloneustes* loved to eat hard, solid food, such as ammonites.

SAUROPTERYGIAN EOSAUROPTERYGIA SUBORDER | 65

Peloneustes

Body size: Approximately 3 meters
Diet: Ammonites
Period of existence: Jurassic
Fossil origin: United Kingdom, Europe

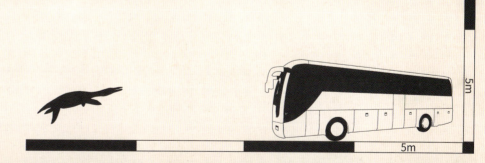

Kronosaurus
The terrifying marine dominator

The *Kronosaurus* and the *Peloneustes* belong to the same family, but their sizes are vastly different.

    The *Kronosaurus* has a body length of nine to ten meters. Its teeth are more than seven centimeters long. Coupling with great speed, it can easily catch whatever prey it wants. The *Kronosaurus* was once thought to be the largest member of the *Pliosauridae* family. Although another family member eventually took that title away, the *Kronosaurus* is still a terrifying dominator.

Millions of Years Ago	252.17 ±0.06	~247.2	~237		201.3 ±0.2		174.1 ±1.0	163.5 ±1.0
Epoch	Early Triassic	Middle Triassic		Late Triassic		Early Jurassic		Middle Jurassic
Period	Triassic					Jurassic		
Era								
Eon								

SAUROPTERYGIAN EOSAUROPTERYGIA SUBORDER | **67**

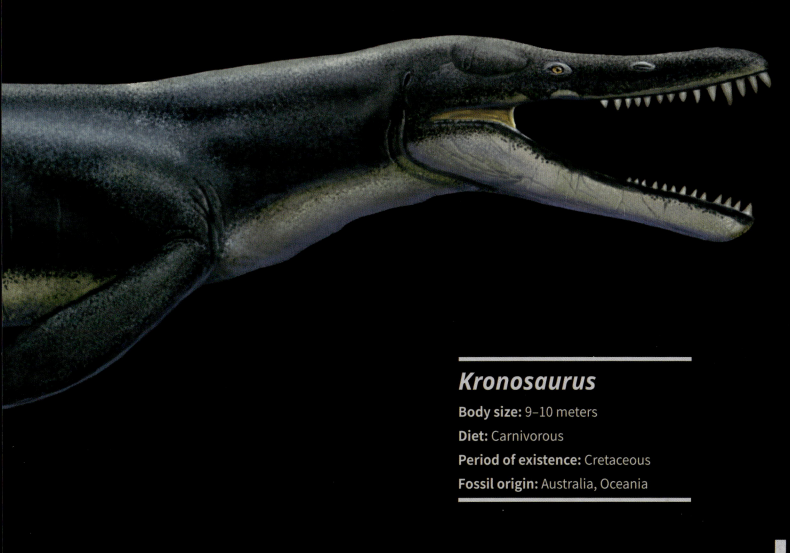

Kronosaurus

Body size: 9–10 meters
Diet: Carnivorous
Period of existence: Cretaceous
Fossil origin: Australia, Oceania

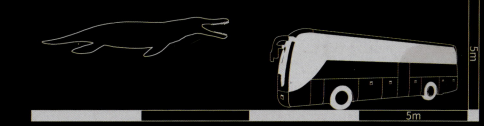

Brachauchenius

Body size: Approximately 6–9 meters
Diet: Carnivorous
Period of existence: Cretaceous
Fossil origin: North America and South America

SAUROPTERYGIAN EOSAUROPTERYGIA SUBORDER | 69

Brachauchenius
A witness of the extinction of the plesiosaurs

Not even the most ferocious can hope to escape death. When the *Brachauchenius* appeared, it didn't know the species would have a short life. The fierce *Brachauchenius* didn't have much time to make a name for itself. Before long it perished, along with all members of the *Plesiosauridae* family, meekly exiting from the stage of life.

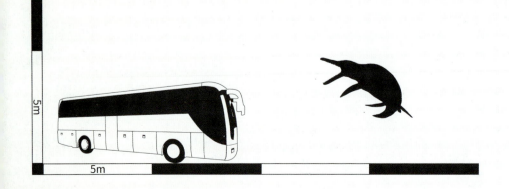

Polycotylus

Body size: Approximately 5 meters
Diet: Fish
Period of existence: Cretaceous
Fossil origin: North America and Europe

SAUROPTERYGIAN EOSAUROPTERYGIA SUBORDER | 71

A *Polycotylus*
hunts for ammonites

The beautiful ocean is also a stage showing the hunters against the hunted. Now, we see a *Polycotylus* chasing after a small ammonite.

The *Polycotylus* looks like something in between the long-necked Plesiosaurs and the short-necked Pliosaurs. It has a large head, a rounded back, and a short, thick neck. It has broad flippers, which allow it to be a fast predator in the sea. Once it has sights on prey, it is sure to make a catch.

A *Liopleurodon*
hunts a *Eustreptospondylus*

The weather is scorching hot, and a *Eustreptospondylus* wants to visit a river for a cool, refreshing drink. It has no way of knowing that a twelve-meter *Liopleurodon* is leisurely resting on the river bed, waiting for prey to present itself.

Soon, the *Liopleurodon* has its wish granted, when the *Eustreptospondylus* is about to lower its head down into the river. The *Liopleurodon* dashes out from the water and viciously bites into the *Eustreptospondylus*. It is too late for the *Eustreptospondylus* to resist!

The *Liopleurodon* is a member of the *Pliosauridae* family. It is not only a good swimmer but also has an extremely keen sense of smell, which it uses to locate food and danger.

Liopleurodon

Body size: 7–10 meters
Diet: Carnivorous
Period of existence: Jurassic
Fossil origin: France, United Kingdom, and Russia, Europe

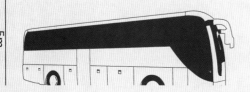

SAUROPTERYGIAN EOSAUROPTERYGIA SUBORDER | 73

74 | PNSO ENCYCLOPEDIA FOR CHILDREN THE SECRETS OF ANCIENT SEA MONSTERS

Yuzhoupliosaurus

Body size: Approximately 4 meters
Diet: Fish
Period of existence: Jurassic
Fossil origin: China, Asia

SAUROPTERYGIAN EOSAUROPTERYGIA SUBORDER | 75

Preferring fresh water
Yuzhoupliosaurus

When reptiles returned from land to water, not all of them lived in the sea. For example, the *Yuzhoupliosaurus* preferred freshwater.

The *Yuzhoupliosaurus* is about four meters long and has a relatively short neck. It uses its five pairs of large teeth and twenty-three or twenty-four pairs of smaller ones to hunt.

Macroplata
The sprinting champion in the sea

If someone held a one-hundred-meter race in the ocean, the *Macroplata* would easily win, because it can dash with tremendous speed in a short burst.

The *Macroplata*'s teeth are sharp, extending out from its mouth to form a crisscross pattern. These teeth allow *Macroplata* to prey on slippery fish with ease.

Millions of Years Ago	252.17 ±0.06	~247.2	~237	201.3 ±0.2	174.1 ±1.0	163.5 ±1.0
Epoch	Early Triassic	Middle Triassic	Late Triassic	Early Jurassic	Middle Jurassic	
Period	Triassic			Jurassic		
Era						
Eon						

SAUROPTERYGIAN EOSAUROPTERYGIA SUBORDER | 77

Macroplata

Body size: Approximately 4.5 meters
Diet: Fish
Period of existence: Jurassic
Fossil origin: Europe

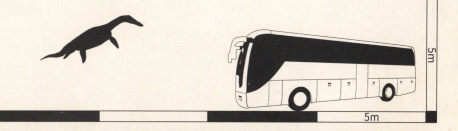

Origins of Archosauria Fossils

Compiled by: PNSO

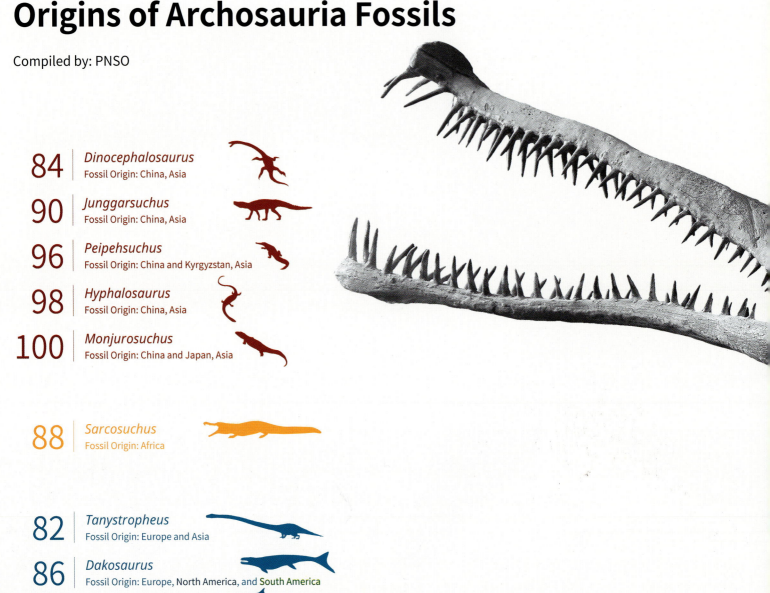

84 | *Dinocephalosaurus*
Fossil Origin: China, Asia

90 | *Junggarsuchus*
Fossil Origin: China, Asia

96 | *Peipehsuchus*
Fossil Origin: China and Kyrgyzstan, Asia

98 | *Hyphalosaurus*
Fossil Origin: China, Asia

100 | *Monjurosuchus*
Fossil Origin: China and Japan, Asia

88 | *Sarcosuchus*
Fossil Origin: Africa

82 | *Tanystropheus*
Fossil Origin: Europe and Asia

86 | *Dakosaurus*
Fossil Origin: Europe, North America, and South America

94 | *Metriorhynchus*
Fossil Origin:
United Kingdom, France, and Germany, Europe

92 | *Armadillosuchus*
Fossil Origin: Brazil, South America

Asia | South America | Africa | Europe | North America | Oceania

Peipehsuchus fossil

Period of Existence of Archosauria Fossils in the Mesozoic Era

Compiled by: PNSO

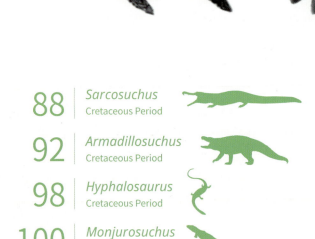

82 | *Tanystropheus*
Triassic Period

84 | *Dinocephalosaurus*
Triassic Period

86 | *Dakosaurus*
Late Jurassic to Early Cretaceous

88 | *Sarcosuchus*
Cretaceous Period

90 | *Junggarsuchus*
Jurassic Period

92 | *Armadillosuchus*
Cretaceous Period

94 | *Metriorhynchus*
Jurassic Period

98 | *Hyphalosaurus*
Cretaceous Period

96 | *Peipehsuchus*
Jurassic Period

100 | *Monjurosuchus*
Cretaceous Period

Millions of Years Ago	252.17 ±0.06	~247.2	~237		201.3 ±0.2		174.1 ±1.0	163.5 ±1.0
Epoch	Early Triassic	Middle Triassic	Late Triassic		Early Jurassic		Middle Jurassic	
Period		Triassic				Jurassic		
Era								
Eon								

Sarcosuchus fossil

~145.0		100.5		66.0
Late Jurassic	Early Cretaceous		Late Cretaceous	
		Cretaceous		
Mesozoic				
Phanerozoic Eon				

Tanystropheus
It has a super long neck!

ARCHOSAURIA PROTOROTHYRIDIDAE FAMILY | 83

The incredibly long neck of the *Tanystropheus* accounts for half of its six-meter-long body. Although its long neck looks impressive, it also slows it down. The *Tanystropheus* is clumsy in water, having difficulty even turning its body. When hunting for fish, however, its long neck is helpful. The *Tanystropheus* can use its long neck to get close to its prey, without the latter seeing its full body and being scared away. When its prey has any chance to realize the predator nearby, it is too late.

Tanystropheus

Body size: Approximately 6 meters
Diet: Fish
Period of existence: Triassic
Fossil origin: Europe and Asia

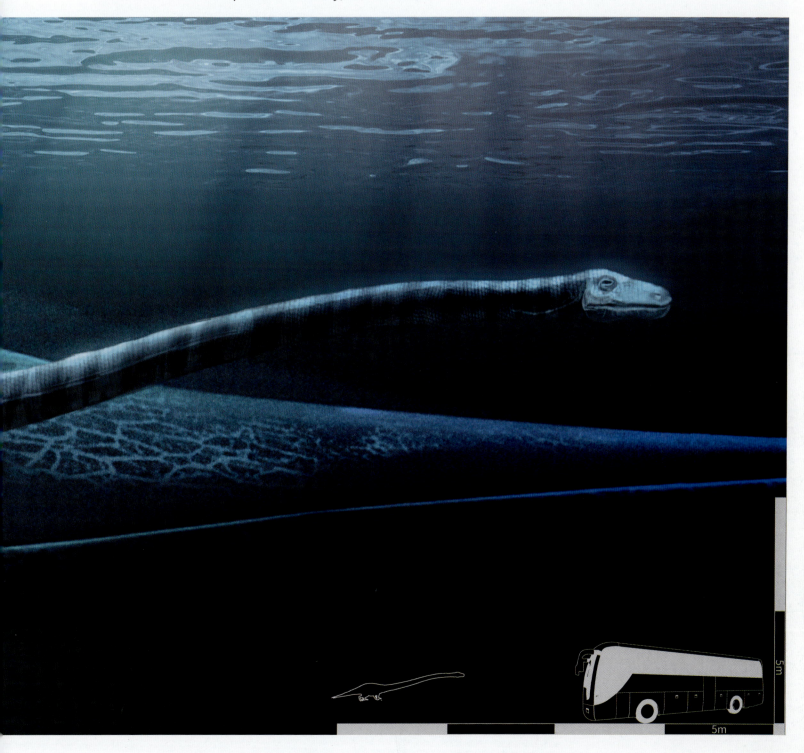

ARCHOSAURIA PROTOROTHYRIDIDAE FAMILY | 85

Dinocephalosaurus
A "vacuum cleaner" in water

The *Dinocephalosaurus* is a scary-looking marine reptile; its long neck makes it look like a vacuum cleaner. When it opens its gigantic mouth, it sucks up all the smaller creatures around it in an instant to make a meal. It has sharp and staggered teeth that can catch fish easily.

The *Dinocephalosaurus* lives in the shallow waters of the ocean. It has adapted well to living in water.

Dinocephalosaurus

Body size: Approximately 2.7 meters
Diet: Fish
Period of existence: Triassic
Fossil origin: China, Asia

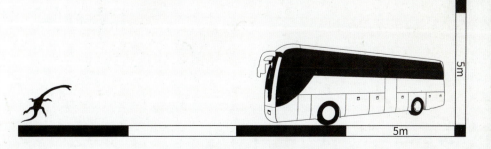

Dakosaurus
A large, fierce-looking mouth

Almost all members of the Thalattosuchia (sea crocodile) suborder have a small head and a long, narrow mouth, but the *Dakosaurus* is different.

The *Dakosaurus* comes from the same suborder, but it has a giant head and a ferocious-looking mouth. They are never contented with feeding on small fish and shrimp. If they are lucky, they will happily devour a *Platypterygius* whole.

Dakosaurus

Body size: 4–5 meters
Diet: Carnivorous
Period of existence: Late Jurassic to Early Cretaceous
Fossil origin: Europe, North America, and South America

Paulwin the *Dakosaurus* reconstructed model (1:50)

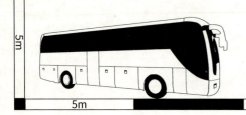

A *Sarcosuchus* attacks a *Suchomimus*

The vast ocean is full of beastly creatures; after seeing the *Dakosaurus*, now behold the terrifying *Sarcosuchus*!

The *Sarcosuchus* is one of the largest crocodile mimics. This enormous creature is as large as a bus. Its back is covered in armored plates, the largest of which can reach one meter. No one dares to get close to the *Sarcosuchus*. With its wide jaw and 132 sharp, thick teeth, it is strong enough to conquer just about any prey. Look, right now the *Sarcosuchus* has set its sights on a *Suchomimus*. There is no question that it will mercilessly slaughter the large but unfortunate prey.

Sarcosuchus

Body size: 8–12 meters
Diet: Carnivorous
Period of existence: Cretaceous
Fossil origin: Africa

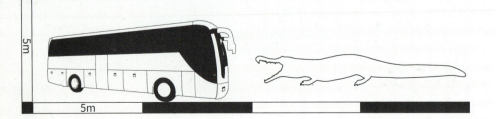

ARCHOSAURIA CROCODYLOMORPHA SUPERORDER | 89

A fast runner
Junggarsuchus

Have you ever seen a crocodile with four long legs? Have you ever seen a crocodile that runs fast? Well, come and look at this one!

The *Junggarsuchus* is an ancestor of the modern-day crocodile, but it looks quite different from the ones we see today. The *Junggarsuchus* doesn't crawl on its stomach; instead, its long legs allowed it to stand above the ground, like dinosaurs. In addition, the *Junggarsuchus* can run quickly, nothing like the slow, plodding crocodiles.

Millions of Years Ago	252.17 ±0.06	~247.2		~237		201.3 ±0.2		174.1 ±1.0		163.5 ±1.0
Epoch	Early Triassic	Middle Triassic			Late Triassic		Early Jurassic		Middle Jurassic	
Period				Triassic				Jurassic		
Era										
Eon										

ARCHOSAURIA CROCODYLOMORPHA SUPERORDER | 91

Junggarsuchus

Body size: Less than 1 meter
Diet: Carnivorous
Period of existence: Jurassic
Fossil origin: China, Asia

The *Armadillosuchus* that lives on land

The *Armadillosuchus* is not really a prehistoric aquatic reptile, because it is an entirely terrestrial creature, meaning it spends all its time on the land. Still, it belongs to the Crocodyliformes clade, so we take some time to introduce this special guy.

The *Armadillosuchus*'s body structure is different from other Crocodyliformes to adapt a terrestrial life. Its teeth share many characteristics with mammalians, and its body armor is like that of modern-day armadillos. Those big differences make it unlike the other members of its group.

Armadillosuchus

Body size: Approximately 2 meters
Diet: Carnivorous
Period of existence: Cretaceous
Fossil origin: Brazil, South America

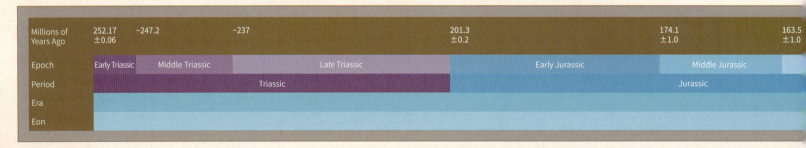

ARCHOSAURIA CROCODYLOMORPHA SUPERORDER | 93

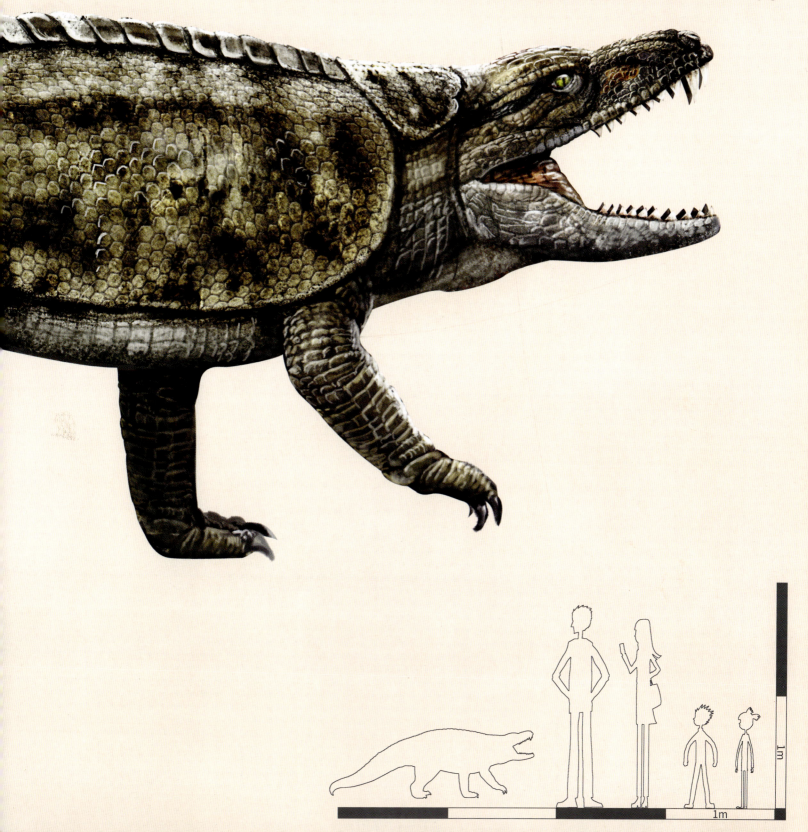

Late Jurassic
Early Cretaceous
Cretaceous
Late Cretaceous
Mesozoic
Phanerozoic Eon

Metriorhynchus
A defenseless sea crocodile

The *Metriorhynchus* is a type of Thalattosuchia (sea crocodile). It is roughly three meters and looks surprisingly like the modern-day crocodile. Most members of the sea crocodiles have their bodies covered with hard scales to defend against predators, but the *Metriorhynchus* has none. Its defenseless, slippery body allows it to adapt better to living in the water.

Metriorhynchus

Body size: Approximately 3 meters
Diet: Fish and Plesiosaurs' babies
Period of existence: Jurassic
Fossil origin: United Kingdom, France, and Germany, Europe

96 | PNSO ENCYCLOPEDIA FOR CHILDREN THE SECRETS OF ANCIENT SEA MONSTERS

Peipehsuchus

Body size: Approximately 3 meters
Diet: Fish
Period of existence: Jurassic
Fossil origin: China and Kyrgyzstan, Asia

Millions of Years Ago	252.17 ±0.06	~247.2	~237		201.3 ±0.2		174.1 ±1.0
Epoch	Early Triassic	Middle Triassic	Late Triassic		Early Jurassic		Middle Jurassic
Period	Triassic				Jurassic		
Era							
Eon							

ARCHOSAURIA CROCODYLOMORPHA SUPERORDER | 97

The *Peipehsuchus*
that loves eating fish

The *Peipehsuchus* is an extinct sea crocodile. It is a unique-looking creature, with a long and pointed mouth, which is full of razor-sharp teeth. Its back is covered with hard, rigid scales. The *Peipehsuchus* is fond of eating fish.

Hyphalosaurus
Living in the lakes

Unlike the marine reptiles, the slender *Hyphalosaurus* prefers the lakes, where it hunts freshwater fish and shrimp.

The *Hyphalosaurus* looks like a smaller version of the Nothosaurs; its lean, streamlined body is well-suited to living in the water. The most notable feature is its long neck.

Hyphalosaurus

Body size: 0.8–1.1 meters
Diet: Fish and shrimp
Period of existence: Cretaceous
Fossil origin: China, Asia

Monjurosuchus
A common creature in Liaoxi, China

The *Monjurosuchus* and the *Hyphalosaurus* are both members of the Choristodera order. Their forelimbs look like oars, which work perfectly with their flat tail to propel them forward in the water. Compared with the slender body of the *Hyphalosaurus*, the *Monjurosuchus* is chubbier. Its large head, short limbs, and thick neck give it a clumsy look.

The *Monjurosuchus* family flourished in Liaoxi, China, during the Cretaceous period. Moreover, scientists have discovered fossils of this creature in Japan.

Monjurosuchus
Body size: 0.4 meters
Diet: Carnivorous
Period of existence: Cretaceous
Fossil origin: China and Japan, Asia

Origins of Squamata Fossils

Compiled by: PNSO

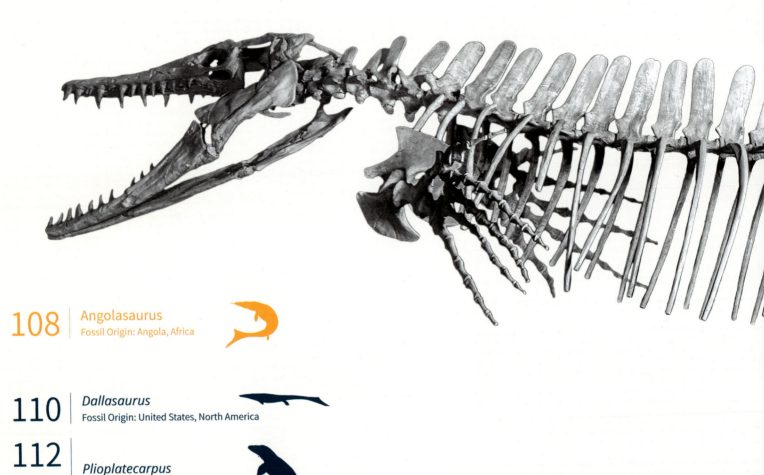

108	*Angolasaurus* Fossil Origin: Angola, Africa	
110	*Dallasaurus* Fossil Origin: United States, North America	
112 **114**	*Plioplatecarpus* Fossil Origin: North America and Europe	
116	*Clidastes* Fossil Origin: United States, North America	
118	*Selmsaurus* Fossil Origin: United States, North America	
122	*Plotosaurus* Fossil Origin: United States, North America	
126	*Tylosaurus* Fossil Origin: North America, Europe, and Africa	
128	*Globidens* Fossil Origin: North America, South America, Africa, Europe, and Asia	

■ Asia　　■ South America　　■ Africa　　■ Europe　　■ North America　　■ Oceania

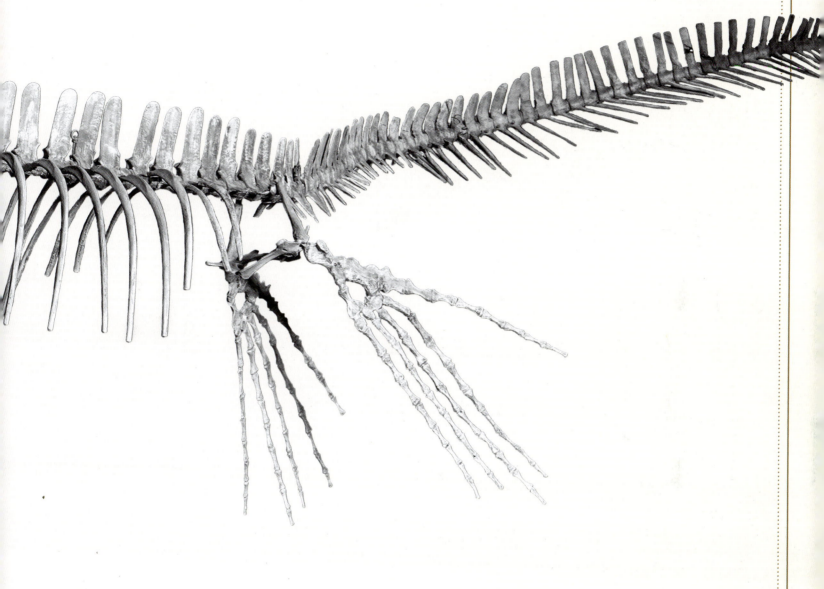

Mosasaur fossil

106	*Aigialosaurus* Fossil Origin: Croatia, Europe
120	*Hainosaurus* Fossil Origin: Belgium and Netherlands, Europe
124	*Mosasaurus* Fossil Origin: Europe, North America, Asia, and Africa

Period of Existence of Squamata Fossils in the Mesozoic Era

Compiled by: PNSO

106 | *Aigialosaurus* — Cretaceous Period
108 | *Angolasaurus* — Cretaceous Period
110 | *Dallasaurus* — Cretaceous Period
112 | *Plioplatecarpus* — Cretaceous Period
114 |
116 | *Clidastes* — Cretaceous Period
118 | *Selmsaurus* — Cretaceous Period
120 | *Hainosaurus* — Cretaceous Period
122 | *Plotosaurus* — Cretaceous Period
124 | *Mosasaurus* — Cretaceous Period
126 | *Tylosaurus* — Cretaceous Period
128 | *Globidens* — Cretaceous Period

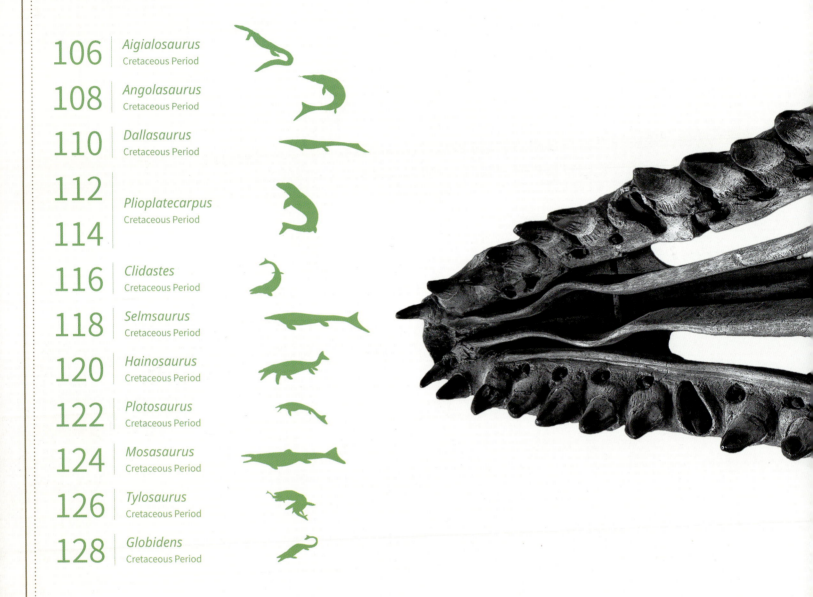

Millions of Years Ago	252.17 ±0.06	~247.2	~237		201.3 ±0.2		174.1 ±1.0	163.5 ±1.0
Epoch	Early Triassic	Middle Triassic		Late Triassic		Early Jurassic		Middle Jurassic
Period			Triassic				Jurassic	
Era								
Eon								

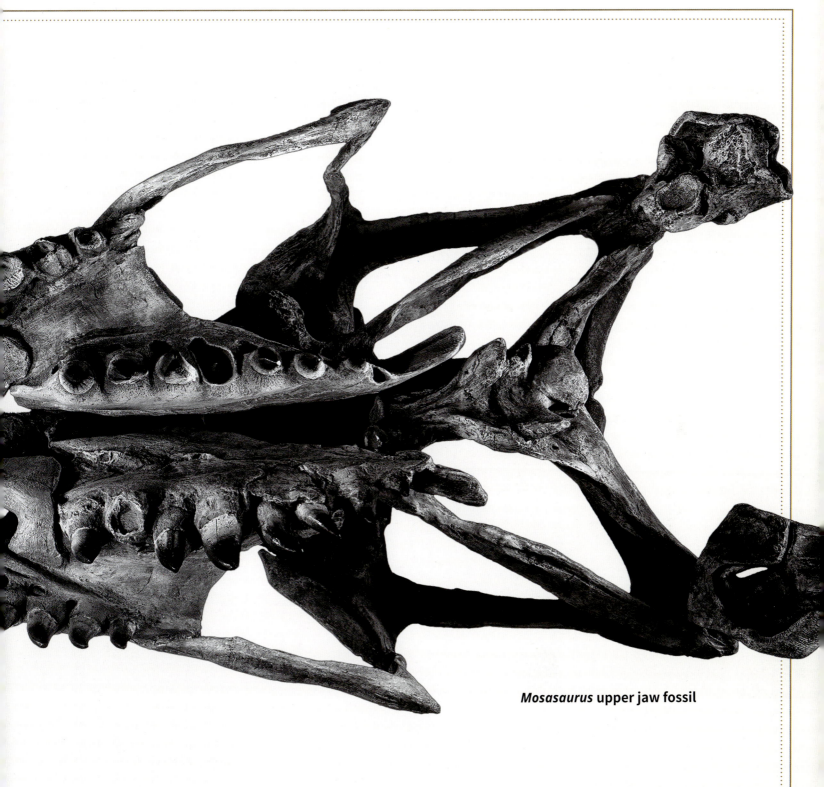

Mosasaurus upper jaw fossil

Aigialosaurus
The ancestor of the *Mosasaurus*!

The petite *Aigialosaurus* probably doesn't attract your attention, but it is the ancestor of the ferocious *Mosasaurus*. Members of the Mosasauroidea superorder are known for their slender, snake-like bodies, as well as the reputation of being some of the most ferocious animals ever seen in the ocean. When they first appeared, they were quite similar to lizards; however, over millions of years of evolution, they have become the fierce overlords of the ocean, with a body length of more than ten meters.

Looking at an *Aigialosaurus*, you may think that it doesn't look well-suited to living in the water. But if you look carefully at its smooth, flat tail, you can see that it has the right tool; by swinging its large, wide tail, it can propel itself to move through the water.

Aigialosaurus

Body size: Approximately 1.5 meters
Diet: Fish
Period of existence: Cretaceous
Fossil origin: Croatia, Europe

Angolasaurus
Founder of Mosasaurs

The *Angolasaurus* is among the founders of the *Mosasauridae* family. It is slender, with a slim head full of sharp teeth. It is about five to seven meters long, smaller than many of its neighbors. Still, at the time when it was born, it was bigger than most of its relatives. It is a good swimmer and moves forward quickly by twisting into an "S" shape and swinging its body.

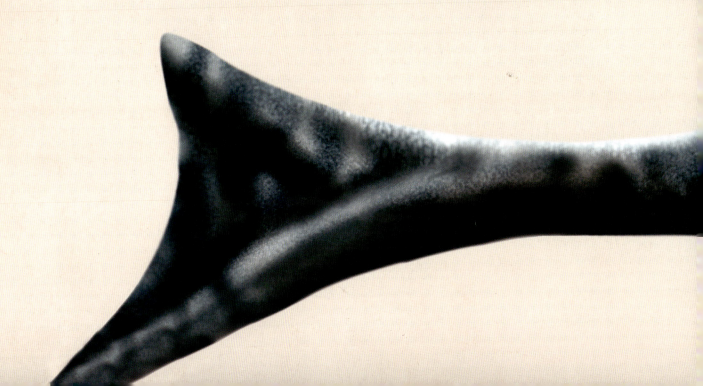

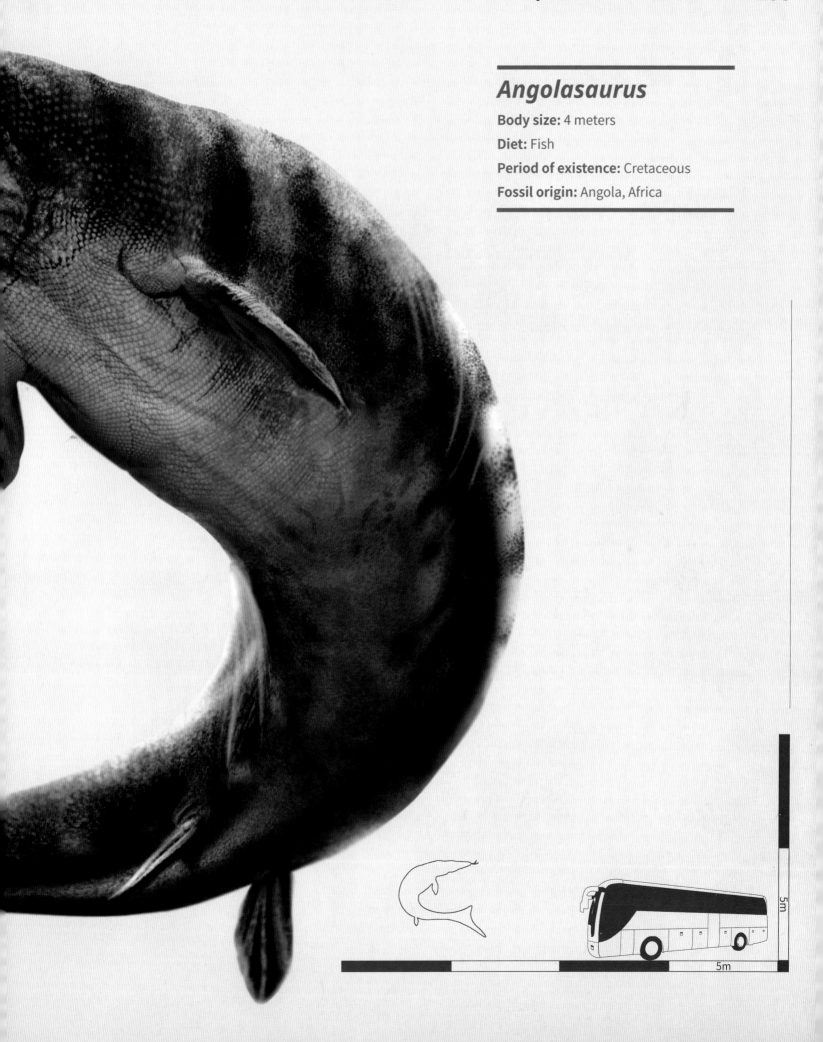

Angolasaurus

Body size: 4 meters
Diet: Fish
Period of existence: Cretaceous
Fossil origin: Angola, Africa

Dallasaurus
The smallest Mosasaur

The first Mosasaurs were small, and the *Dallasaurus* is particularly so. With a body length of roughly one meter, it is undoubtedly the smallest member of the *Mosasauridae* family.

The *Dallasaurus* is an amphibian, spending part of its time on land. Even so, their shortened limbs indicate that they are trying to adapt to living in the water.

Although the *Dallasaurus*'s body is thin and slender, it has developed a broad, flat tail fin. This is another piece of evidence that suggests the *Dallasaurus* is adapting.

Dallasaurus

Body size: Approximately 1 meter
Diet: Carnivorous
Period of existence: Cretaceous
Fossil origin: United States, North America

Plioplatecarpus

It can swallow prey wider than its head!

The *Plioplatecarpus*'s beautiful, triangular head seems small, and its mouth narrow. Why, then, is it able to swallow prey larger than its little head? Well, the *Plioplatecarpus*'s lower jaw is flexible because a joint allows its mouth to open widely, so it can swallow prey much larger than itself, like a snake does.

Plioplatecarpus

Body size: 4.5–7.5 meters
Diet: Cephalopods
Period of existence: Cretaceous
Fossil origin: North America and Europe

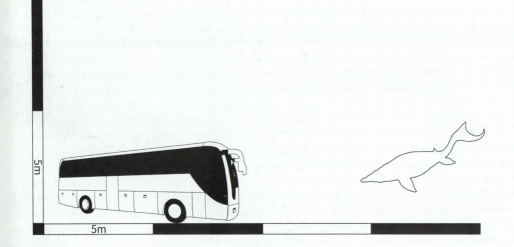

A pregnant Plioplatecarpus

The *Plioplatecarpus* has a peculiar jaw, but that is only part of the reason for being famous; it is also one of the most precious fossils to have ever been discovered. In 1996, American scientists in the state of South Dakota discovered a well-preserved *Plioplatecarpus* fossil that contained an embryo. This meant that they found a fossil of a pregnant *Plioplatecarpus*. To discover such a fossil was rare indeed, as it could provide us with more information about how the *Mosasauridae* family reproduced.

Plioplatecarpus

Body size: Approximately 6 meters
Diet: Carnivorous
Period of existence: Cretaceous
Fossil origin: North America and Europe

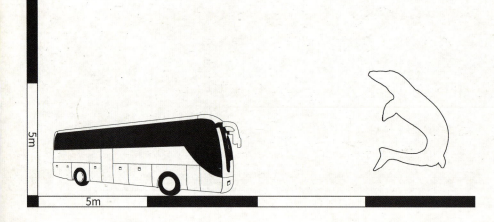

Clidastes
What a great swimmer!

The *Clidastes*'s size is modest, with an average body length of only two to four meters, even the longest is just above six meters. However, it is an exceptionally good swimmer—you only need to take one look at its large, flat tail, to understand how it propels itself forward in the water with such power. Thanks to its speed, the *Clidastes* survives in an environment full of strong predators.

The *Clidastes* had a long, slender body, and it enjoys preying on fish and birds near the sea's surface.

Clidastes

Body size: 2–6.2 meters
Diet: Fish and birds
Period of existence: Cretaceous
Fossil origin: United States, North America

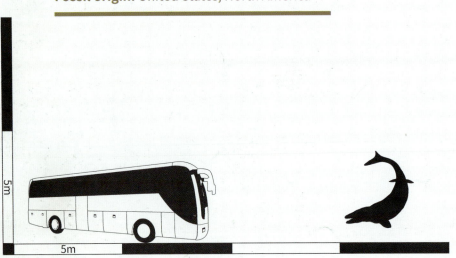

Selmasaurus
It can't get its mouth to open any wider

Most of the *Mosasauridae* family members can gobble up enormous prey, an action possible due to their flexible lower jaw. The *Selmasaurus*, however, doesn't have this structure. When facing larger prey, it drools with envy but can't attack.

The *Selmasaurus* is modestly sized, with a long, slender body. It lives in the shallow waters in the sea, preying on fish and other small animals.

Selmasaurus

Body size: Approximately 3 meters
Diet: Fish
Period of existence: Cretaceous
Fossil origin: United States, North America

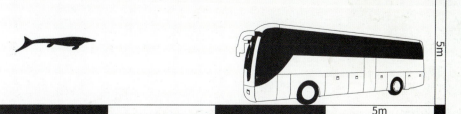

Hainosaurus
A huge appetite

The earliest descriptions of the *Hainosaurus* called it a seventeen-meter gigantic marine beast. Further research led scientists to believe that it is roughly twelve meters long. Still, it is one of the largest members of the *Mosasauridae* family and sits atop the ocean's food chain.

In order to support their enormous bodies, the *Hainosaurus* haves a huge appetite and eats practically anything it finds. Paleontologists once examined a *Hainosaurus* fossil, and in its stomach, they found the remains of Plesiosaurs, *Archelon*, other Mosasaurs, and even dinosaurs. This means that *Hainosaurus* must have been a formidable eater.

SQUAMATA MOSASAUROIDEA SUPERFAMILY | 121

Hainosaurus

Body size: Approximately 12.2 meters
Diet: Carnivorous
Period of existence: Cretaceous
Fossil origin: Belgium and Netherlands, Europe

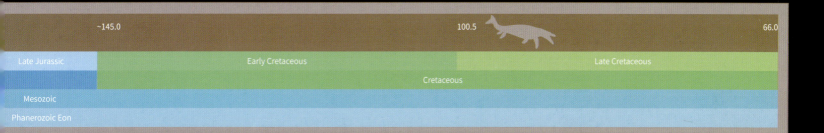

Plotosaurus

The most advanced marine reptile

After a long period of evolution, members of the *Mosasauridae* family have developed bodies well adapted to living in the ocean. The *Plotosaurus*, which has experienced remarkable physical changes, is one such example and may well be called the most advanced marine reptile.

If you take a closer look, you will notice that its flippers are thin and slender, like those of the modern-day dolphin. These allow for fast swimming. With a mouth full of crooked, uneven teeth, once it gets hold of prey, the hold will be inescapable. Finally, the *Plotosaurus* has a tail, which provided it with a great amount of power to propel itself forward. All these useful features make the *Plotosaurus* one of the most dominant creatures in the ocean.

SQUAMATA MOSASAUROIDEA SUPERFAMILY 123

Plotosaurus

Body size: 9–13 meters
Diet: Fish, shellfish, and squid
Period of existence: Cretaceous
Fossil origin: United States, North America

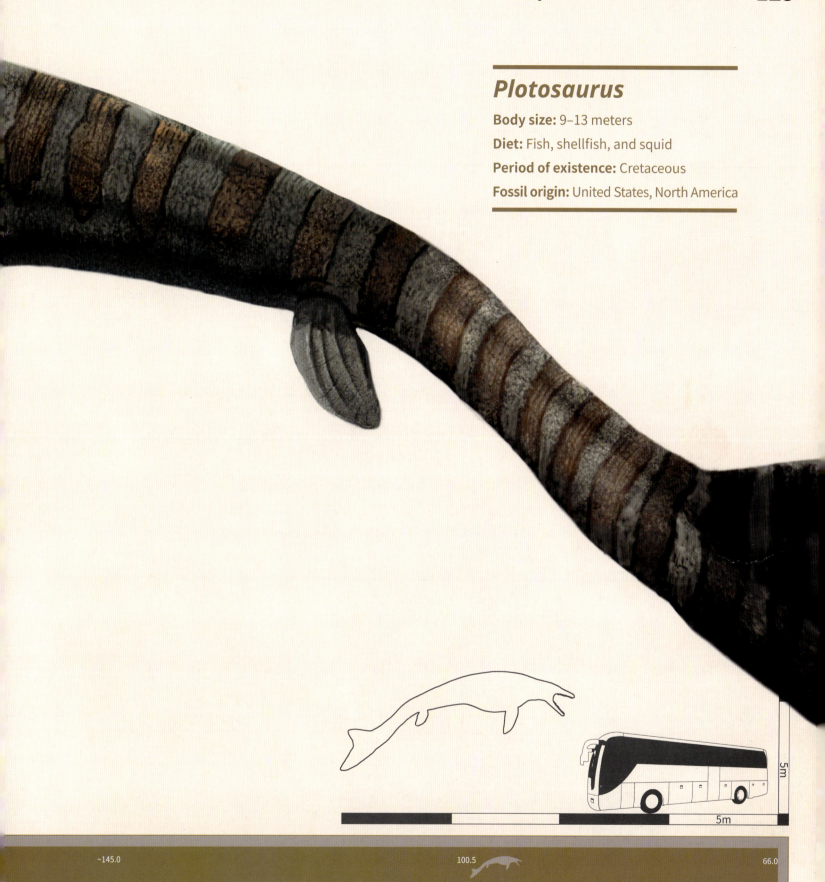

A *Mosasaurus*
hunting an *Archelon*

The *Mosasaurus* was the most powerful creature to ever live in the ocean. It can reach a maximum length of over seventeen meters. It has an enormous, strong head, powerful jaws that could bite into anything, and razor-sharp teeth which can easily break open hard shells. The *Mosasaurus* preys on just about everything that lives in the ocean, including fish, ammonites, sea turtles, and even other small members of the *Mosasauridae* family. It has a streamlined body, and a strong tail, well-suited to living in the ocean. The *Mosasaurus* is one of the overlords of the ocean, and if it lives to the present day, even the fiercest sharks cannot hope to rival it.

Right now, this terrifying *Mosasaurus* is devouring an *Archelon*, the poor creature's blood staining the ocean dark crimson.

Mosasaurus

Body size: 12–17.6 meters
Diet: Carnivorous
Period of existence: Cretaceous
Fossil origin: Europe, North America, Asia, and Africa

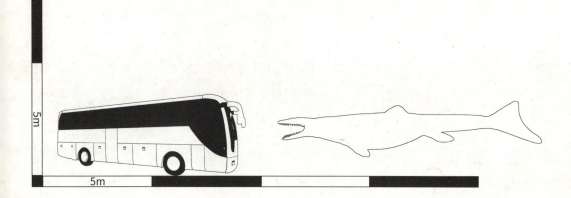

A *Tylosaurus*
preying on a small *Mosasaurus*

Although the adult *Mosasaurus* rules the ocean, a young *Mosasaurus* can often end up becoming its enemy's next meal.

Look at this unlucky little *Mosasaurus*; it has only just left its mother and now falls into the clutches of a terrifying *Tylosaurus*. The little *Mosasaurus* fearfully calls out for its mother, but the *Tylosaurus* won't wait for any help to come; it has taken a bite and is ready to devour the little *Mosasaurus* right now!

The *Tylosaurus* is a giant Mosasaur, one of the largest members of the *Mosasauridae* family. That's why it has the strength to attack a small *Mosasaurus*.

Tylosaurus

Body size: Approximately 15 meters
Diet: Carnivorous
Period of existence: Cretaceous
Fossil origin: North America, Europe, and Afric

The *Globidens*
with unusual teeth

The *Globidens*'s teeth are unusual. Two types of teeth exist in its mouth: those in the front of its mouth are cone-shaped, whilst others in the back are spherical. The unusual teeth seem to be perfectly suited for eating crustaceans; the conical teeth can pierce through the hard upper shell of a crustacean, and its spherical teeth can crush its exoskeleton. In fact, scientists have found plenty of the remains of crustaceans in their stomachs!

Globidens
Body size: 5.5–6 meters
Diet: Crustaceans
Period of existence: Cretaceous
Fossil origin: North America, South America, Africa, Europe, and Asia

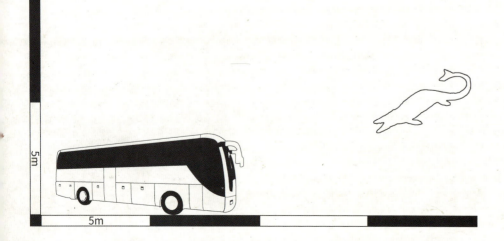

SQUAMATA MOSASAUROIDEA SUPERFAMILY | 129

Origins of Ichthyopterygia Fossils

Compiled by: PNSO

148 *Utatsusaurus*
Fossil Origin: Japan, Asia

150 *Chaohusaurus*
Fossil Origin: China, Asia

160 *Mixosaurus*
Fossil Origin: Asia, Europe, and North America

162 *Qianichthyosaurus*
Fossil Origin: China, Asia

152 *Shastasaurus*
Fossil Origin: North America and Asia

156 *Californosaurus*
Fossil Origin: United States, North America

158 *Cymbospondylus*
Fossil Origin: North America, Europe, Asia, South America, and Oceania

164 *Shonisaurus*
Fossil Origin: United States, North America

146 *Ichthyosaurus*
Fossil Origin: United Kingdom, Europe

154 *Besanosaurus*
Fossil Origin: Italy, Europe

166 *Stenopterygius*
Fossil Origin: United Kingdom and Italy, Europe

168 *Excalibosaurus*
Fossil Origin: United Kingdom, Europe

170 *Eurhinosaurus*
Fossil Origin: United Kingdom and Germany, Europe

175 *Platypterygius*
Fossil Origin: Europe, South America, North America, and Oceania

172 *Ophthalmosaurus*
Fossil Origin: Europe, North America, and South America

 Asia   South America   Africa   Europe   North America   Oceania

Temnodontosaurus fossil

Period of Existence of Ichthyopterygia Fossils in the Mesozoic Era

Compiled by: PNSO

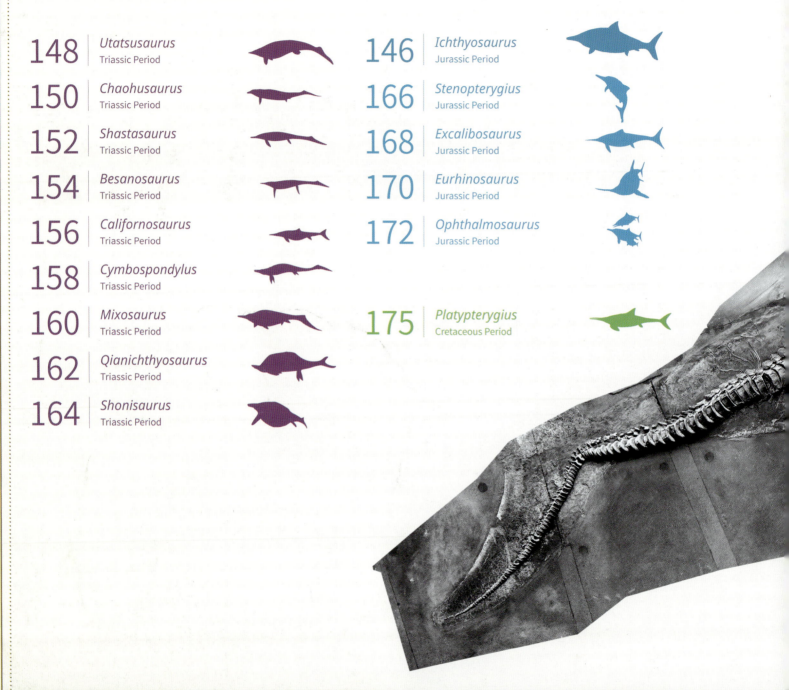

Ichthyosaurus fossil

Ichthyosaurus
revealing the mystery in the ocean

Out of all of the reptiles that left the land to return to the sea, one family looked like modern-day fish or dolphins. Most of them were not large, but through struggling, some of them eventually rose to the highest position in the ocean. They ruled over the ocean world for millions of years, until the arrival of Plesiosaurs, after which they slowly faded away. These were the Ichthyosaurs.

The *Ichthyosaurus* is the typical representative of the Ichthyosaurs. They have long and slender heads, large eyes, and a beautifully streamlined body. They swim fast and are fond of eating squid.

ICHTHYOPTERYGIA SUPERORDER | 135

Ichthyosaurus

Body size: 2–5 meters
Diet: Squid
Period of existence: Jurassic
Fossil origin: United Kingdom, Europe

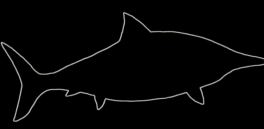
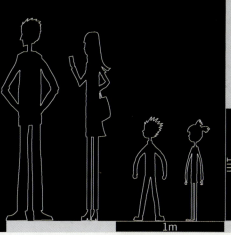

Dancing in water
Utatsusaurus

The *Utatsusaurus* was one of the earliest members of the *Ichthyosauridae* family. It was not large. On its streamlined body, there is a small tail fin. When it swims, it moves forward by swinging its body from side to side, as if dancing elegantly. The *Utatsusaurus* has short teeth, which are not good enough to take on large prey, so it usually eats small fish.

Utatsusaurus

Body size: Approximately 1.5–3 meters
Diet: Fish
Period of existence: Triassic
Fossil origin: Japan, Asia

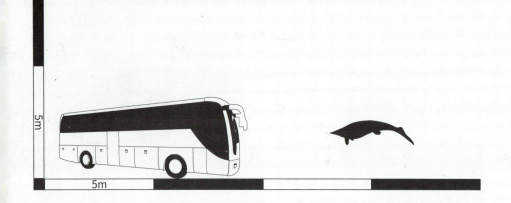

The large-eyed
Chaohusaurus

The *Chaohusaurus* is also one of the earliest members of the *Ichthyosauridae* family. It has flippers and a tail fin, necessary gadgets for swimming, but these are too small to have much use in water. Because of this, it is likely that the *Chaohusaurus* moves slowly in water.

Fortunately, the *Chaohusaurus* has a pair of large eyes, which allow it to see its surroundings well. In this way, it anticipates danger and gets away before enemies get too close.

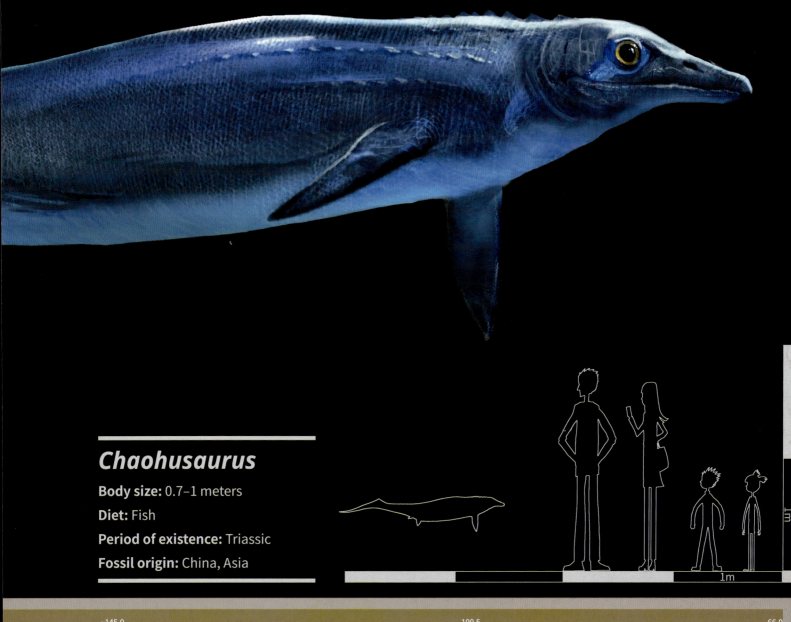

Chaohusaurus

Body size: 0.7–1 meters
Diet: Fish
Period of existence: Triassic
Fossil origin: China, Asia

Shastasaurus
Is it the largest Ichthyosaurus?

People used to think that the *Shastasaurus* is only an average-sized member of the *Ichthyosauridae* family. But paleontologists found an enormous *Shastasaurus* fossil in Canada, one that reached twenty-one meters. If this discovery is accurate, the *Shastasaurus* is the largest member of the *Ichthyosauridae* family!

Most Ichthyosaurs have slender snouts and mouths full of teeth. The *Shastasaurus*, however, has a short snout and no teeth. Because of this, the food they eat is different from the other members of the *Ichthyosauridae* family. They prefer small fish and shell-less cephalopods.

ICHTHYOPTERYGIA SUPERORDER | 141

Shastasaurus

Body size: 4–8 meters, in certain cases reaching up to 21 meters
Diet: Fish and shell-less cephalopods
Period of existence: Triassic
Fossil origin: North America and Asia

Besanosaurus
Spreading its offspring around the world

The *Besanosaurus* doesn't seem well-suited to swimming fast. It has no dorsal fin, and its tail fin is small. However, this doesn't stop them from becoming a dominant species in the ocean. They had become a top predator family by focusing on growing in numbers. In a short period of time, they successfully established themselves as a thriving family.

Millions of Years Ago	252.17 ±0.06	~247.2	~237		201.3 ±0.2	174.1 ±1.0	163.5 ±1.0
Epoch	Early Triassic	Middle Triassic		Late Triassic		Early Jurassic	Middle Jurassic
Period	Triassic					Jurassic	
Era							
Eon							

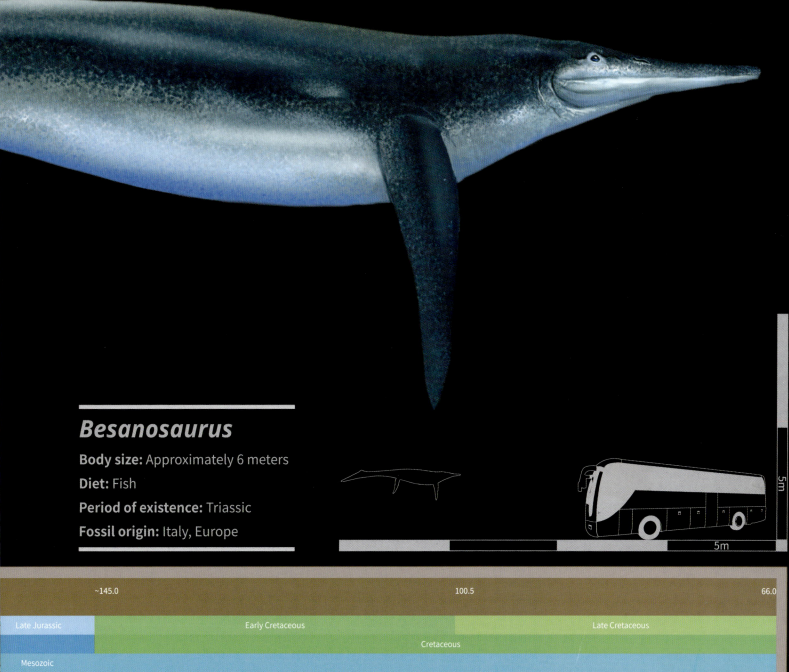

Besanosaurus

Body size: Approximately 6 meters
Diet: Fish
Period of existence: Triassic
Fossil origin: Italy, Europe

Californosaurus
It has dorsal fins!

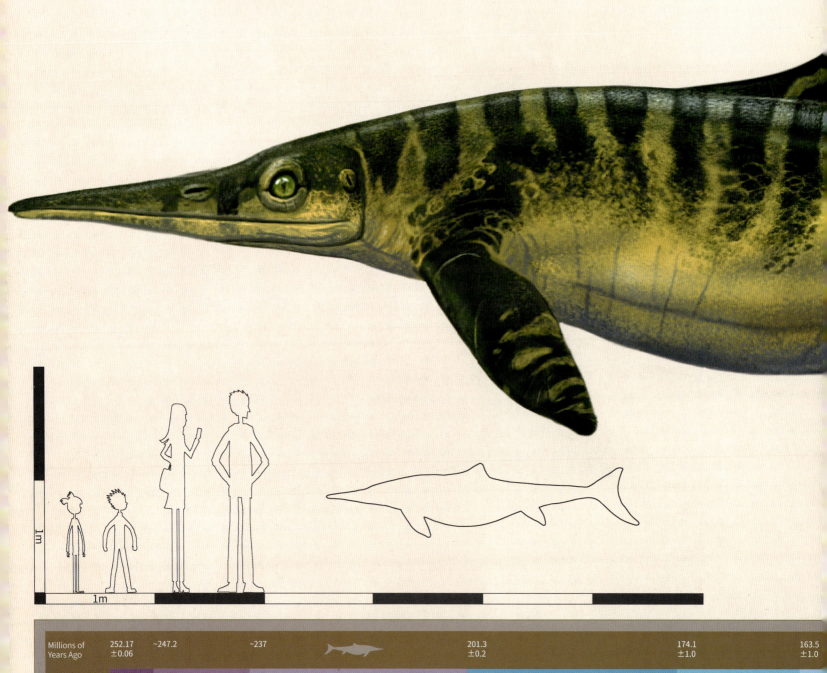

ICHTHYOPTERYGIA SUPERORDER | 145

Finding a dorsal fin on the back of a modern-day marine animal is common, but for the early marine reptiles, it was a rare feature. The *Californosaurus* was a species that tried to develop one. Before they emerged, a typical early member of the *Ichthyosauridae* family had no dorsal fin, only a tiny tail fin, and a body that looked like a lizard; however, the *Californosaurus* radically changed that. It looked much more like the modern-day dolphin and was well-adapted to life in the ocean.

Californosaurus

Body size: Approximately 3 meters
Diet: Fish and shrimp
Period of existence: Triassic
Fossil origin: United States, North America

Cymbospondylus
Master of the sea in the Triassic

During the Triassic period, the *Cymbospondylus* was one of the ocean's most dominant creatures, and the species flourished throughout the entire world.

The *Cymbospondylus* has a slender body, a relatively straight tail, and a modest tail fin. Its back is bare, without any dorsal fin. The *Cymbospondylus* looks quite different from the dolphin-like Ichthyosaurs of later periods. Instead, it is more like an eel.

Cymbospondylus

Body size: 6–10 meters
Diet: Fish
Period of existence: Triassic
Fossil origin: North America, Europe, Asia, South America, and Oceania

The *Mixosaurus*
with its diamond-shaped tail fin

The *Mixosaurus* is one of the earlier members of the *Ichthyosauridae* family, but it looks modern. It has a rounded body, four flippers, and a unique tail fin. Unlike most of its friends, which have triangular tail fins, the *Mixosaurus* has a diamond-shaped tail fin, which can propel itself to move strongly forward.

The *Mixosaurus* has excellent eyesight, which is useful for seeing clearly in the darkness of the deep ocean. It can easily spot its prey and watch out for enemies lurking nearby.

ICHTHYOPTERYGIA SUPERORDER | 149

Mixosaurus

Body size: 1 meter
Diet: Fish
Period of existence: Triassic
Fossil origin: Asia, Europe, and North America

A *Qianichthyosaurus*
chases a small fish

A withered tree branch falls with great force into the water, causing a string of bubbles to rise to the surface. It is the Triassic period in present-day Guizhou, China. A *Qianichthyosaurus* with enormous eyes swims through a cluster of ammonites, its gigantic mouth wide open as it chases a small, frightened fish.

The fish is barely big enough to be an appetizer for the *Qianichthyosaurus*. However, the *Qianichthyosaurus* is never picky; it chases after each prey with the same concentration and effort.

Qianichthyosaurus
Body size: 2–3 meters
Diet: Fish and squid
Period of existence: Triassic
Fossil origin: China, Asia

ICHTHYOPTERYGIA SUPERORDER | 151

Shonisaurus
A "submarine" in the sea

The setting sun casts a shimmer on the water's surface, giving it a ruby-like deep crimson color. A group of *Shonisaurus* is swimming through the water, scaring away creatures foraging for food.

The *Shonisaurus* is roughly fifteen meters. Once, researchers thought that they found fossils of the *Shonisaurus* reaching up to twenty-one meters, but they later contended that those fossils were in fact of a type of *Shastasaurus*. Nevertheless, the *Shonisaurus* is still a giant in the *Ichthyosauridae* family. It uses its slender flippers to move forward in water to search for prey, its imposing figure like a submarine.

Shonisaurus
Body size: Approximately 15 meters
Diet: Carnivorous
Period of existence: Triassic
Fossil origin: United States, North America

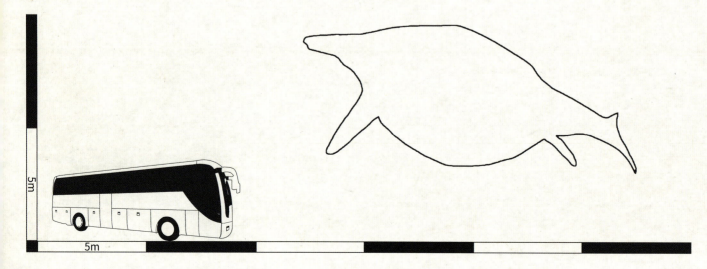

ICHTHYOPTERYGIA SUPERORDER | 153

A *Stenopterygius* leaping out of the water

The sunshine is lovely today. A *Stenopterygius* jumps out of the water to feel what it is like outside of the sea.

The *Stenopterygius* has a small, round body, like that of a dolphin. However, it also has a long tail and a large tail fin. When it swings its tail from side to side, it propels itself forward. The *Stenopterygius* relies on its speed to come out on top in fierce competitions. Scientists speculate that the *Stenopterygius* had a swimming speed close to that of modern-day tuna, one of the fastest fish.

Stenopterygius

Body size: 2–4 meters
Diet: Fish
Period of existence: Jurassic
Fossil origin: United Kingdom and Germany, Europe

ICHTHYOPTERYGIA SUPERORDER | 155

Excalibosaurus
Mouth shaped like a sword

The *Excalibosaurus* enjoys moving around in the deep ocean because its excellent eyesight allows it to see clearly in the murky depths. Its most unusual feature is not the eyesight, however. Have you noticed its strange-looking mouth? The *Excalibosaurus* is proud of its sharp and narrow upper beak, which is four times longer than its lower beak. This sword-like beak is an excellent tool in hunting.

Excalibosaurus

Body size: Approximately 6 meters
Diet: Shellfish
Period of existence: Jurassic
Fossil origin: United Kingdom and Germany, Europe

Millions of Years Ago	252.17 ±0.06	~247.2	~237	201.3 ±0.2	174.1 ±1.0	163.5 ±1.0
Epoch	Early Triassic	Middle Triassic	Late Triassic	Early Jurassic	Middle Jurassic	
Period	Triassic			Jurassic		
Era						
Eon						

ICHTHYOPTERYGIA SUPERORDER | 157

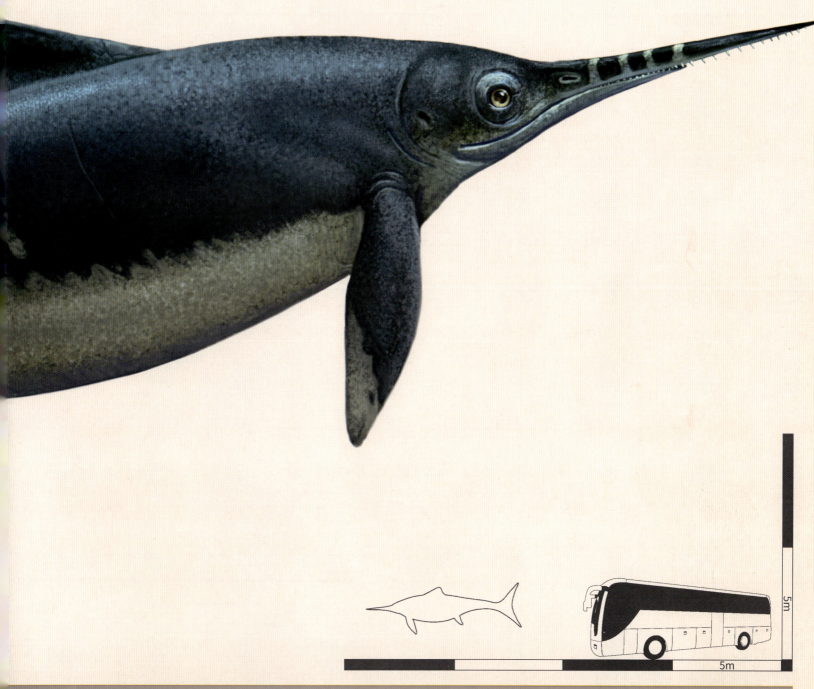

~145.0	100.5	66.0
Late Jurassic	Early Cretaceous	Late Cretaceous
	Cretaceous	
Mesozoic		
Phanerozoic Eon		

Eurhinosaurus
Samurai of the sea

The *Eurhinosaurus* and the *Excalibosaurus* are from the same family. Therefore, it is natural that the *Eurhinosaurus* also has a long upper beak, a weapon it can wield like a samurai. Despite having this powerful weapon, it is usually not violent. When the *Eurhinosaurus* is dining, it prefers to do it gracefully, like a gentleman. The *Eurhinosaurus* prefers not to rip its prey apart. Instead, it usually uses the beak to stir up the sediment around its prey, forcing them to run out. In that confusion, the *Eurhinosaurus* then ruthlessly gobbles them up.

Eurhinosaurus

Body size: More than 6 meters
Diet: Shellfish
Period of existence: Jurassic
Fossil origin: Europe

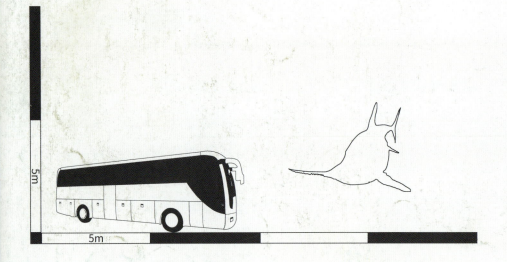

Ophthalmosaurus
It has huge eyes!

In the pitch-black darkness of the deep sea, a family of three *Ophthalmosaurus* is returning home.

The *Ophthalmosaurus* has large eyes, with a diameter of roughly twenty-two centimeters. In comparison, the human eye has a diameter of about two and a half centimeters. Thanks to the large eyes, the *Ophthalmosaurus* sees well when it is hunting in the dark depths of the ocean, or during the night, when few other predators are around to snatch away its food. The *Ophthalmosaurus* has no teeth, so it prefers to eat squid and other creatures, which it can swallow in one big gulp.

Ophthalmosaurus
Body size: 4–6 meters
Diet: Squid
Period of existence: Jurassic
Fossil origin: Europe, North America, and South America

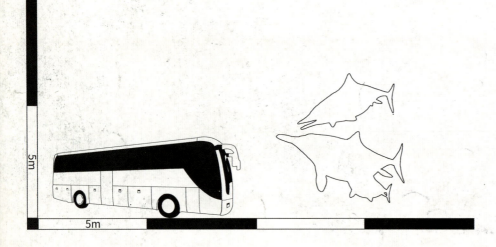

ICHTHYOPTERYGIA SUPERORDER | 163

A *Platypterygius*
hunting an *Archelon*

After a group of *Platypterygius* has laid their eggs, they pick an *Archelon* as a target and gang up on it.

The *Platypterygius* is like a medium-sized, beautifully streamlined dolphin. Its mouth is full of sharp teeth. It can capture fish, squid, waterfowl, and even *Archelon* with ease.

The *Platypterygius* was the last member of the *Ichthyosauridae* family. It witnessed the tragic demise of the *Ichthyosauridae* family.

Platypterygius

Body size: Approximately 7 meters
Diet: Fish and squid
Period of existence: Cretaceous
Fossil origin: Europe, South America, North America, and Oceania

Index

A
Aigialosaurus / 106
Angolasaurus / 108
Anshunsaurus / 16
Armadillosuchus / 92
Askeptosaurus / 12
B
Besanosaurus / 142
Bishanopliosaurus / 62
Brachauchenius / 68
C
Californosaurus / 144
Ceresiosaurus / 34
Chaohusaurus / 138
Cimoliasaurus / 46
Clidastes / 116
Cryptoclidus / 52
Cymbospondylus / 146
D
Dakosaurus / 86
Dallasaurus / 110
Dinocephalosaurus / 84
E
Elasmosaurus / 58
Eretmosaurus / 40
Eurhinosaurus / 158
Excalibosaurus / 156
F

G
Globidens / 128
H
Hainosaurus / 120
Hyphalosaurus / 98
I
Ichthyosaurus / 134
J
Junggarsuchus / 90
K
Kaiwhekea / 56
Kronosaurus / 66
L
Lariosaurus / 30
Lariosaurus xingyiensis / 32
Liopleurodon / 72
M
Macroplata / 76
Metriorhynchus / 94
Mixosaurus / 148
Monjurosuchus / 100
Mosasaurus / 124
Muraenosaurus / 42
N
Nothosaurus giganteus / 28
O
Ophthalmosaurus / 160

P
Peipehsuchus / 96
Peloneustes / 64
Pistosaurus / 36
Placochelys / 16
Placodus / 20
Platypterygius / 162
Plesiosaurus / 50
Plioplatecarpus / 112
Plotosaurus / 122
Polycotylus / 70
Psephochelys / 24
Psephoderma / 22
Q
Qianichthyosaurus / 150
R
Rhomaleosaurus / 48
S
Sarcosuchus / 88
Shastasaurus / 140
Shonisaurus / 152
Sinocyamodus / 18
Stenopterygius / 154
Styxosaurus / 60
T
Tanystropheus / 82
Trinacromerum / 44
Tylosaurus / 126

U
Utatsusaurus / 136
V
W
Woolungasaurus / 54
X
Y
Yunguisaurus / 38
Yuzhoupliosaurus / 74
Z

Reference

1. Liu, J. (1999). "Sauropterygian from Triassic of Guizhou, China." *Chinese Science Bulletin* 44 (14): 1312–1316.

2. Liu, J., and O. Rieppel. (2005). "Restudy of Anshunsaurus huangguoshuensis (Reptilia: Thalattosauria) from the Middle Triassic of Guizhou, China." *American Museum Novitates* 3488: 1–34.

3. Rieppel, O., J. Liu, and C. Li. (2006). "A new species of the thalattosaur genus Anshunsaurus (Reptilia: Thalattosauria) from the Middle Triassic of Guizhou Province, southwestern China." *Vertebrata PalAsiatica* 44: 285–296.

4. Cheng, L., X. Chen, and C. Wang. (2007). "A New Species of Late Triassic Anshunsaurus (Reptilai: Thalattosauria) from Guizhou Province." *ACTA Geologica Sinica* 81: 1–7.

5. Li, C. (2000). "Placodont (Reptilia: Placodontia) from Upper Triassic of Guizhou, southwest China." *Vertebrata PalAsiatica* 38 (4): 314–317.

6. Dayong, Jiang, Ryosuke Motani, Hao Weicheng, Olivier Rieppel, Sun Yuanlin, Lars Schmitz, and Sun Zuoyu. (2008). "First record of Placodontoidea (Reptilia, Sauropterygia, Placodontia) from the Eastern Tethys." *Journal of Vertebrate Paleontology* 28 (3): 904–908.

7. Rieppel, O. (1995). "The genus Placodus: systematics, morphology, paleobiogeography, and paleobiology." *Fieldiana Geology*, new series 31: 1–44.

8. Diedrich, C. J. (2010). "Palaeoecology of Placodus gigas (Reptilia) and other placodontids—Middle Triassic macroalgae feeders in the Germanic basin of central Europe—and evidence for convergent evolution with Sirenia." *Palaeogeography, Palaeoclimatology, Palaeoecology* 285: 287–306.

9. Li, C. (2002). "A new cyamodontoid placodont from Triassic of Guizhou, China." *Chinese Science Bulletin* 47 (5): 403.

10. Diedrich, C. (2009). "The vertebrates of the Anisian/Ladinian boundary (Middle Triassic) from Bissendorf (NW Germany) and their contribution to the anatomy, palaeoecology, and palaeobiogeography of the Germanic Basin reptiles." *Palaeogeography, Palaeoclimatology, Palaeoecology* 273 (1): 1–16.

11. Rieppel, O. (1994). "The status of the sauropterygian reptile Nothosaurus juvenilis from the Middle Triassic of Germany." *Paleontology* 37: 733–745.

12. Shang, Q.-H. (2007). "New information on the dentition and tooth replacement of Nothosaurus (Reptilia: Sauropterygia)." *Palaeoworld* 16: 254–263.

13. Albers, P. C. H. (2005). "A new specimen of Nothosaurus marchicus with features that relate the taxon to Nothosaurus winterswijkensis." *Vertebrate Palaeontology* 3 (1): 1–7.

14. Klein, N., and P. C. H. Albers. (2009). "A new species of the sauropsid reptile Nothosaurus from the Lower Muschelkalk of the western Germanic Basin, Winterswijk, The Netherlands." *Acta Palaeontologica Polonica* 54 (4): 589–598.

15. Rieppel, O., J.-M. Mazin, and E. Tchernov. (1997). "Speciation along rifting continental margins: a new Nothosaur from the Negev (Israul)." *Comptes Rendus de l'Académie des Sciences Series IIA* 325 (12): 991–997.

16. Jingling, L., and O. Rieppel. (2004). "A new nothosaur from Middle Triassic of Guizhou, China." *Vertebrata PalAsiatica* 42 (1): 1–12.

17. Rieppel, Olivier, Li Jinling, and Jun Liu. (2003). "Lariosaurus xingyiensis (Reptilia: Sauropterygia) from the Triassic of China." *Canadian Journal of Earth Sciences* 40 (4): 621–634.

18. Hugi, Jasmina. (2011). "The long bone histology of Ceresiosaurus (Sauropterygia, Reptilia) in comparison to other eosauropterygians from the Middle Triassic of Monte San Giorgio (Switzerland/Italy)." *Swiss Journal of Palaeontology* 130 (2): 297–306.

19. Rieppel, Olivier. (1998). "The status of the sauropterygian reptile genera Ceresiosaurus, Lariosaurus, and Silvestrosaurus from the Middle Triassic of Europe." *Fieldiana Geology*, new series 38: 1–46.

20. Ketchum, Hilary F., and Roger B. J. Benson. (2011). "A new pliosaurid (Sauropterygia, Plesiosauria) from the Oxford Clay Formation (Middle Jurassic, Callovian) of England: evidence for a gracile, longirostrine grade of Early-Middle Jurassic pliosaurids." *Special Papers in Palaeontology* 86: 109–129.

21. Cheng, Yen-Nien, Tamaki Sato, Xiao-Chun Wu, and Chun Li. (2006). "First complete pistosauroid from the Triassic of China." *Journal of Vertebrate Paleontology* 26 (2): 501–504.

22. Sato, Tamaki, Li-Jun Zhao, Xiao-Chun Wu, and Chun Li. (2013). "A new specimen of the Triassic pistosauroid Yunguisaurus, with implications for the origin of Plesiosauria (Reptilia, Sauropterygia)." *Palaeontology* 57 (1).

23. Brown, David S., and Nathalie Bardet. (1994). "Plesiosaurus rugosus Owen, 1840 (currently Eretmosaurus rugosus; Reptilia, Plesiosauria): proposed designation of a neotype." *Bulletin of Zoological Nomenclature* 51 (3): 247–249.

24. Wilhelm, B. C. (2010). "A New Partial Skeleton of a Cryptocleidoid Plesiosaur from the Upper Jurassic Sundance Formation of Wyoming." *Journal of Vertebrate Paleontology* 30 (6): 1736–1742.

25. O'Keefe, F. R., and W. Wahl. (2003). "Current taxonomic status of the plesiosaur Pantosaurus striatus from the Upper Jurassic Sundance Formation, Wyoming." *Paludicola* 4 (2): 37–46.

26. O'Keefe, F. R. (2001). "Ecomorphology of plesiosaur flipper geometry." *Journal of Evolutionary Biology* 14 (6): 987–991.

27. Zammit, M. (2008). "Elasmosaur (Reptilia: Sauropterygia) neck flexibility: Implications for feeding strategies." *Comparative Biochemistry and Physiology Part A: Molecular & Integrative Physiology* 150 (2): 124–130.

28. O'Keefe, F. Robin, and Hallie P. Street. (2009). "Osteology of the Cryptoclidoid Plesiosaur Tatenectes laramiensis, With Comments on the Taxonomic Status of the Cimoliasauridae." *Journal of Vertebrate Paleontology* 29 (1): 48–57.

29. Smith, Adam S., and Gareth J. Dyke. (2008). "The skull of the giant predatory pliosaur Rhomaleosaurus cramptoni: implications for plesiosaur phylogenetics." *Naturwissenschaften* 95: 975–980.

30. Benson, Roger B. J., Hilary F. Ketchum, Leslie F. Noè, and Marcela Gґmez-Pґrez. (2011). "New information on Hauffiosaurus (Reptilia, Plesiosauria) based on a new species of the Alum Shale Member (Lower Toarcian: Lower Jurassic) of Yorkshire, UK." *Palaeontology* 54 (3): 547–571.

31. Smith, Adam S., and Peggy Vincent. (2010). "A new genus of pliosaur (Reptilia: Sauropterygia) from the Lower Jurassic of Holzmaden, Germany." *Palaeontology* 53 (5): 1049–1063.

32. Larkin, Nigel, Sonia O'Connor, and Dennis Parsons. (2010). "The virtual and physical preparation of the Collard plesiosaur from Bridgwater Bay, Somerset, UK." *Geological Curator* 9 (3): 107.

33. Cheng, Y.-N., X.-C. Wu, and Q. Ji. (2004). "Chinese marine reptiles gave live birth to young." *Nature* 423: 383–386.

34. Kubo, Tai, Mark T. Mitchell, and Donald M. Henderson. (2012). "Albertonectes vanderveldei, a new elasmosaur (Reptilia, Sauropterygia) from the Upper Cretaceous of Alberta." *Journal of Vertebrate Paleontology* 32(3): 557–572.

35. Cruickshank, A. R. I., P. G. Small, and M. A. Taylor. (1991). "Dorsal nostrils and hydrodynamically driven underwater olfaction in plesiosaurs." *Nature* 352: 62–64.

36. O'Keefe, F. R., and L. M. Chiappe. (2011). "Viviparity and K-Selected Life History in a Mesozoic Marine Plesiosaur (Reptilia, Sauropterygia)." *Science* 333 (6044): 870–873.

37. O'Gorman, J. P., and Z. Gasparini. (2013). "Revision of Sulcusuchus erraini (Sauropterygia, Polycotylidae) from the Upper Cretaceous of Patagonia, Argentina." *Alcheringa* 37: 161–174.

38. Brown, David S., and Arthur R. I. Cruickshank. (1994). "The skull of the Callovian plesiosaur Cryptoclidus eurymerus, and the sauropterygian cheek." *Palaeontology* 37.4: 941.

39. Benson, R. B. J., M. Evans, and P. S. Druckenmiller. (2012). "High Diversity, Low Disparity and Small Body Size in Plesiosaurs (Reptilia, Sauropterygia) from the Triassic–Jurassic Boundary." *PLoS ONE* 7 (3), edited by Carles Lalueza-Fox: e31838.

40. Cruickshank, Arthur R. I., and R. Ewan Fordyce. (2002). "A new marine reptile (Sauropterygia) from New Zealand: further evidence for a Late Cretaceous austral radiation of cryptoclidid plesiosaurs." *Palaeontology* 45 (3): 557–575.

41. Ketchum, H. F., and R. B. J. Benson. (2010). "Global interrelationships of Plesiosauria (Reptilia, Sauropterygia) and the pivotal role of taxon sampling in determining the outcome of phylogenetic analyses." *Biological Reviews* 85: 361–392.

42. Carpenter, K. (1999). "Revision of North American elasmosaurs from the Cretaceous of the western interior." *Paludicola* 2 (2): 148–173.

43. Carpenter, K. (2003). "Vertebrate Biostratigraphy of the Smoky Hill Chalk (Niobrara Formation) and the Sharon Springs Member (Pierre Shale)." *High-Resolution Approaches in Stratigraphic Paleontology* 21: 421–437.

44. Sachs, S. (2004). "Redescription of Woolungasaurus glendowerensis (Plesiosauria: Elasmosauridae) from the Lower Cretaceous of Northeast Queensland." *Memoirs of the Quennsland Museum* 49: 215–233.

45. Sachs, S. (2005). "Redescription of Elasmosaurus platyurus, Cope 1868 (Plesiosauria: Elasmosauridae) from the Upper Cretaceous (lower Campanian) of Kansas, USA." *Paludicola* 5(3): 92–106.

46. Sato, Tamaki. (2003). "Terminonatator ponteixensis, a new elasmosaur (Reptilia:Sauropterygia) from the Upper Cretaceous of Saskatchewan." *Journal of Vertebrate Paleontology* 23(1): 89–103.

47. Williston, S. W. (1890). "Structure of the Plesiosaurian Skull." *Science* 16 (405): 262.

48. Kear, B. P. (2003). "Cretaceous marine reptiles of Australia: a review of taxonomy and distribution." *Cretaceous Research* 24: 277–303.

49. Romer, A. S., and A. D. Lewis. (1959). "A mounted skeleton of the giant plesiosaur Kronosaurus." *Breviora* 112: 1–15.

50. Sachs S. (2005). "Tuarangisaurus australis sp. nov. (Plesiosauria: Elasmosauridae) from the Lower Cretaceous of northeastern Queensland, with additional notes on the phylogeny of the Elasmosauridae." *Memoirs of the Queensland Museum* 50 (2): 425–440.

51. Schumacher, B. A., K. Carpenter, and M. J. Everhart. (2013). "A new Cretaceous Pliosaurid (Reptilia, Plesiosauria) from the Carlile Shale (middle Turonian) of Russell County, Kansas." *Journal of Vertebrate Paleontology* 33 (3): 613.

52. Hampe, O. (2005). "Considerations on a Brachauchenius skeleton (Pliosauroidea) from the lower Paja Formation (late Barremian) of Villa de Leyva area (Colombia)." *Fossil Record* 8 (1): 37–51.

53. Everhart, M. J. (2007). "Historical note on the 1884 discovery of Brachauchenius lucasi (Plesiosauria; Pliosauridae) in Ottawa County, Kansas." *Transactions of the Kansas Academy of Science* 110 (3/4): 255–258.

54. O'Keefe, F. R. (2004). "On the cranial anatomy of the polycotylid plesiosaurs, including new material of Polycotylus latipinnis, Cope, from Alabama." *Journal of Vertebrate Paleontology* 24 (2): 326–34.

55. Albright, L. B., III, D. D. Gillette, and A. L. Titus. (2007). "Plesiosaurs from the Upper Cretaceous (Cenomanian-Turonian) Tropic Shale of southern Utah, Part 2: Polycotylidae." *Journal of Vertebrate Paleontology* 27 (1): 41–58.

56. Noè, Leslie F., Jeff Liston, and Mark Evans. (2003). "The first relatively complete exoccipital-opisthotic from the braincase of the Callovian pliosaur, Liopleurodon." *Geological Magazine* 140 (4): 479–486.

57. Long, J. H., Jr., J. Schumacher, N. Livingston, and M. Kemp. (2006). "Four flippers or two? Tetrapodal swimming with an aquatic robot." *Bioinspir Biomim* 1: 20–29.

58. Zhang, Y. (1985). "A new plesiosaur from Middle Jurassic of Sichuan Basin." *Vertebrata PalAsiatica* 23: 235–240.

59. Rieppel, O., D. Y. Jiang, N. C. Fraser, W. C. Hao, R. Motani, Y. L. Sun, and Z. Y. Sun. (2010). "Tanystropheus cf. T. longobardicus from the Early Late Triassic of Guizhou Province, Southwestern China." *Journal of Vertebrate Paleontology* 30 (4): 1082–1089.

60. Li, C., O. Rieppel, and M. C. LaBarbera. (2004). "A Triassic Aquatic Protorosaur with an Extremely Long Neck." *Science* 305 (5692): 1931.

61. Buchy, M.-C., W. Stinnesbeck, E. Frey, and A. H. G. Gonzalez. (2007). "First occurrence of the genus Dakosaurus (Crocodyliformes, Thalattosuchia) in the Late Jurassic of Mexico." *Bulletin de la Societe Geologique de France* 178 (5): 391–397.

62. Buchy, M.-C. (2008). "New occurrence of the genus Dakosaurus (Reptilia, Thalattosuchia) in the Upper Jurassic of north-eastern Mexico with comments upon skull architecture of Dakosaurus and Geosaurus." *Neues Jahrbuch für Geologie und Paläontologie, Abhandlungen* 249 (1): 1–8.

63. Cau, Andrea, and Federico Fanti. (2011). "The oldest known metriorhynchid crocodylian from the Middle Jurassic of North-eastern Italy: Neptunidraco ammoniticus gen. et sp. Nov." *Gondwana Research* 19 (2): 550–565.

64. Massare, J. A. (1988). "Swimming capabilities of Mesozoic marine reptiles; implications for method of predation." *Paleobiology* 14 (2): 187–205.

65. Fernnndez, M., and Z. Gasparini. (2000). "Salt glands in a Tithonian metriorhynchid crocodyliform and their physiological significance." *Lethaia* 33: 269–276.

66. Sereno, Paul C., Hans C. E. Larson, Christian A. Sidor, and Boubn Gado. (2001). "The Giant Crocodyliform Sarcosuchus from the Cretaceous of Africa." *Science* 294 (5546): 1516–9.

67. Buffetaut, E., and P. Taquet. (1977). "The Giant Crocodilian Sarcosuchus in the Early Cretaceous of Brazil and Niger." *Paleontology* 20 (1).

68. Webb, G. J. W., and Harry Messel. (1978). "Morphometric Analysis of C. porosus from the North Coast of Arnhem Land, Northern Australia." *Australian Journal of Zoology* 26.

69. Head, J. J. (2001). "Systematics and body size of the gigantic, enigmatic crocodyloid Rhamphosuchus crassidens, and the faunal history of Siwalik Group (Miocene) crocodylians." *Journal of Vertebrate Paleontology* 21 (Supplement to No. 3): 59A.

70. Erickson, G. M., and C. A. Brochu. (1999). "How the 'terror crocodile' grew so big." *Nature* 398 (6724).

71. Clark, James M., Xing Xu, Catherine A. Forster, and Yuan Wang. (2004). "A Middle Jurassic 'sphenosuchian' from China and the origin of the crocodylian skull." *Nature* 430 (7003): 1021–1024.

72. Marinho, Thiago S., and Ismar S. Carvalho. (2009). "An armadillo-like sphagesaurid crocodyliform from the Late Cretaceous of Brazil." *Journal of South American Earth Sciences* 27 (1): 36–41.

73. Forrest, R. (2003). "Evidence for scavenging by the marine crocodile Metriorhynchus on the carcass of a plesiosaur." *Proceedings of the Geologists' Association* 114: 363–366.

74. Gandola, R., E. Buffetaut, N. Monaghan, and G. Dyke. (2006). "Salt glands in the fossil crocodile Metriorhynchus." *Journal of Vertebrate Paleontology* 26 (4): 1009–1010.

75. Li, J. (1993). "A new specimen of Peipehsuchus teleorhinus from Ziliujing formation of Daxian, Sichuan." *Vertebrata PalAsiatica*, 31 (2): 85–94.

76. Gao, K.-Q. and D. T. Ksepka. (2008). "Osteology and taxonomic revision of Hyphalosaurus (Diapsida: Choristodera) from the Lower Cretaceous of Liaoning, China." *Journal of Anatomy* 212 (6): 747–768.

77. Buffetaut, E., J. Li, H. Tong, and H. Zhang. (2006). "A two-headed reptile from the Cretaceous of China." *Biology Letters* 3 (1): 80–81.

78. Hou, L.-H., P.-P. Li, D. T. Ksepka, K.-Q. Gao, and M. A. Norell. (2010). "Implications of flexible-shelled eggs in a Cretaceous choristoderan reptile." *Proceedings of the Royal Society B* 277 (1685): 1235–1239.

79. Smith, J. B., and J. D. Harris. (2001). "A taxonomic problem concerning two diapsid genera from the lower Yixian Formation of Liaoning Province, north-eastern China." *Journal of Vertebrate Paleontology* 21 (2): 389–391.

80. Matsumoto, R., S. E. Evans, and M. Manabe. (2007). "The choristoderan reptile Monjurosuchus from the Early Cretaceous of Japan." *Acta Palaeontologica Polonica* 52 (2): 329–350.

81. Gao, K.-Q., and R. C. Fox. (2005). "A new choristodere (Reptilia: Diapsida) from the Lower Cretaceous of western Liaoning Province, China, and phylogenetic relationships of Monjurosuchidae." *Zoological Journal of the Linnean Society* 145 (3): 427–444.

82. Lindgren, J., and M. Siverson. (2004). "The first record of the mosasaur Clidastes from Europe and its palaeogeographical implications." *Acta Palaeontologica Polonica* 49: 219–234.

83. Leblanc, Aaron R. H., Michael W. Caldwell, and Nathalie Bardet. (2012). "A new mosasaurine from the Maastrichtian (Upper Cretaceous) phosphates of Morocco and its implications for mosasaurine systematics." *Journal of Vertebrate Paleontology* 32 (1): 82–104.

84. Lingham-Soliar, T. (1998). "Unusual death of a Cretaceous giant." *Lethaia* 31: 308–310.

85. Camp, C. L. (1951). "Plotosaurus, a new generic name for Kolposaurus Camp, preoccupied." *Journal of Paleontology* 25: 822.

86. Lindgren, J., J. W. M. Jagt, and M. W. Caldwell. (2007). "A fishy mosasaur: the axial skeleton of Plotosaurus (Reptilia, Squamata) reassessed." *Lethaia* 40: 153–160.

87. Dutchak, Alex R., and Michael W. Caldwell. (2009). "A redescription of Aigialosaurus (= Opetiosaurus) bucchichi (Kornhuber, 1901) (Squamata: Aigialosauridae) with comments on mosasauroid systematics." *Journal of Vertebrate Paleontology* 29 (2): 437–452.

88. Reeder, Tod W., Ted M. Townsend, Daniel G. Mulcahy, Brice P. Noonan, Perry L. Wood, Jr., Jack W. Sites, Jr., and John J. Wiens. (2015). "Integrated analyses resolve conflicts over Squamate reptile phylogeny and reveal unexpected placements for fossil taxa." *PloS ONE* 10 (3): e0118199.

89. Grigoriev, D. V. (2013). "Redescription of Prognathodon lutugini (Squamata, Mosasauridae)." *Proceedings of the Zoological Institute RAS* 317 (3): 246–261.

90. Lindgren, J. (2002). "Tylosaurus ivoensis: a giant mosasaur from the early Campanian of Sweden." *Transactions of the Royal Society of Edinburgh* 105: 73–93.

91. Everhart, M. J. (2002). "New data on cranial measurements and body length of the mosasaur, Tylosaurus nepaeolicus (Squamata; Mosasauridae), from the Niobrara Formation of western Kansas." *Transactions of the Kansas Academy of Science* 105 (1–2): 33–43.

92. Russel, Dale. (1975). "A new species of Globidens from South Dakota, and a review of globidentine mosasaurs." *Fieldiana Geology* 33 (13): 235–256.

93. Lingham-Soliar, T. (1991). "Mosasaurs from the Upper Cretaceous of Niger." *Palaeontology* 34 (3): 653–670.

94. Polcyn, M. J., L. L. Jacobs, A. S. Schulp, and O. Mateus. (2010). "The North African Mosasaur Globidens phosphaticus from the Maastrichtian of Angola." *Historical Biology* 22 (3): 175–185.

95. Mulder, E. W. A. (1999). "Transatlantic latest Cretaceous mosasaurs (Reptilia, Lacertilia) from the Maastrichtian type area and New Jersey." *Geologie en Mijnbouw* 78: 281–300.

96. Harrell, T. L., and J. E. Martin. (2014). "A mosasaur from the Maastrichtian Fox Hills Formation of the northern Western Interior Seaway of the United States and the synonymy of Mosasaurus maximus with Mosasaurus hoffmanni (Reptilia: Mosasauridae)." *Netherlands Journal of Geosciences - Geologie en Mijnbouw* 94: 23.

97. Street, Hallie P., and Michael W. Caldwell. (2014). "Reassessment of Turonian mosasaur material from the 'Middle Chalk' (England, UK), and the status of Mosasaurus gracilis Owen, 1849." *Journal of Vertebrate Paleontology* 34 (5): 1072–1079.

98. Lomax, Dean R. (2010). "An Ichthyosaurus (Reptilia, Ichthyosauria) with gastric contents from Charmouth, England: First report of the genus from the Pliensbachian." *Paludicola* 8 (1): 22–36.

99. Martill, D. M. (1993). "Soupy Substrates: A Medium for the Exceptional Preservation of Ichthyosaurs of the Posidonia Shale (Lower Jurassic) of Germany." *Kaupia - Darmstädter Beiträge zur Naturgeschichte* 2: 77–97.

100. Maisch, Michael W., and Andreas T. Matzke. (2003). "Observations on Triassic ichthyosaurs. Part XII. A new Lower Triassic ichthyosaur genus from Spitzbergen." *Neues Jahrbuch für Geologie und Paläontologie Abhandlungen* 229: 317–338.

101. Qing-Hua, Shang, and Li Chun (2009). "On the occurrence of the ichthyosaur Shastasaurus in the Guanling Biota (Late Triassic), Guizhou, China." *Vertebrata PalAsiatica* 47 (3): 178–193.

102. Nicholls, E. L., and M. Manabe. (2004). "Giant ichthyosaurs of the Triassic - a new species of Shonisaurus from the Pardonet Formation (Norian: Late Triassic) of British Columbia." *Journal of Vertebrate Paleontology* 24 (3): 838–849.

103. Sander, P. M., X. Chen, L. Cheng, and X. Wang. (2011). "Short-Snouted Toothless Ichthyosaur from China Suggests Late Triassic Diversification of Suction Feeding Ichthyosaurs." *PLoS ONE* 6 (5), edited by L. Claessens: e19480.

104. Ji, C., D. Y. Jiang, R. Motani, W. C. Hao, Z. Y. Sun, and T. Cai. (2013). "A new juvenile specimen of Guanlingsaurus (Ichthyosauria, Shastasauridae) from the Upper Triassic of southwestern China." *Journal of Vertebrate Paleontology* 33 (2): 340.

105. Xiaofeng, W., G. H. Bachmann, H. Hagdorn, P. M. Sander, G. Cuny, C. Xiaohong, W. Chuanshang, C. Lide, C. Long, M. Fansong, and X. U. Guanghong. (2008). "The Late Triassic Black Shales of the Guanling Area, Guizhou Province, South-West China: A Unique Marine Reptile and Pelagic Crinoid Fossil Lagerstätte." *Palaeontology* 51: 27.

106. Maisch, M. W. (2010). "Phylogeny, systematics, and origin of the Ichthyosauria - the state of the art." *Palaeodiversity* 3:151–214.

107. Shikama, T., T. Kamei, and M. Murata. (1977). "Early Triassic Ichthyosaurus, Utatsusaurus hataii Gen. et Sp. Nov., from the Kitakami Massif, Northeast Japan." *Science Reports of the Tohoku University Second Series (Geology)* 48 (1–2): 77–97.

108. Chen, Xiaohong, P. Martin Sander, Long Cheng, and Xiaofeng Wang. (2013). "A New Triassic Primitive Ichthyosaur from Yuanan, South China." *Acta Geologica Sinica (English Edition)* 87 (3): 672–677.

109. Young, C. C., and Z. Dong. (1972). "On the Triassic aquatic reptiles of China." *Memoires of the Nanjing Institute of Geology and Paleontology* 9: 1–34.

110. Liezhu, Chen. (1985). "Ichthyosaurs from the lower Triassic of Chao County." *Anhui Regional Geology of China* 15: 139–146.

111. Motani, R., and H. You. (1998). "Taxonomy and limb ontogeny of Chaohusaurus geishanensis (Ichthyosauria), with a note on the allometric equation." *Journal of Vertebrate Paleontology* 18: 533–540.

112. McGowan, C. (1986). "A putative ancestor for the swordfish-like ichthyosaur Eurhinosaurus." *Nature* 322 (6078): 454–456.

113. McGowan, C. (2003). "A new Specimen of Excalibosaurus from the English Lower Jurassic." *Journal of Vertebrate Paleontology* 23 (4): 950–956.

114. Motani, R. (1999). "Phylogeny of the Ichthyopterygia." *Journal of Vertebrate Paleontology* 19 (3): 473–496.

115. Motani, R. (1999). "The skull and Taxonomy of Mixosaurus (Ichthyoptergia)." *Journal of Paleontology* 73: 924–935.

116. Motani, R., H. You, and C. McGowan. (1996). "Eel like swimming in the earliest ichthyosaurs." *Nature* 382: 347–388.

117. Jiang, D. Y., L. Schmitz, R. Motani, W.-C. Hao, and Y.-L. Sun. (2006). "A new mixosaurid ichthyosaur from the Middle Triassic." *Journal of Vertebrate Paleontology* 26: 60–69.

118. Maisch, Michael W. (2008). "Revision der Gattung Stenopterygius Jaekel, 1904 emend. von Huene, 1922 (Reptilia: Ichthyosauria) aus dem unteren Jura Westeuropas." *Palaeodiversity* 1: 227–271.

119. Fischer, V., E. Masure, M. S. Arkhangelsky, and P. Godefroit. (2011). "A new Barremian (Early Cretaceous) ichthyosaur from western Russia." *Journal of Vertebrate Paleontology* 31 (5): 1010–1025.

120. Reisdorf, A. G., M. W. Maisch, and A. Wetzel. (2011). "First record of the leptonectid ichthyosaur Eurhinosaurus longirostris from the Early Jurassic of Switzerland and its stratigraphic framework." *Swiss Journal of Geosciences* 104 (2): 211–224.

ZHAO Chuang and YANG Yang
&
PNSO's Scientific Art Projects Plan: Stories on Earth (2010–2070)

ZHAO Chuang and YANG Yang are two professionals who work together to create scientific art. Mr. ZHAO Chuang, a scientific artist, and Ms. YANG Yang, an author of scientific children's books, started working together when they jointly founded PNSO, an organization devoted to the research and creation of scientific art in Beijing on June 1, 2010. A few months later, they launched Scientific Art Projects Plan: Stories on Earth (2010–2070). The plan uses scientific art to create a captivating, historically accurate narrative. These narratives are based on the latest scientific research, focusing on the complex relationships between species, natural environments, communities, and cultures. The narratives consider the perspectives of human civilizations while exploring Earth's past, present, and future. The PNSO founders plan to spend 60 years to do research and create unique and engaging scientific art and literature for people around the world. They hope to share scientific knowledge through publications, exhibitions, and courses. PNSO's overarching goal is to serve research institutions and the general public, especially young people.

PNSO has independently completed or participated in numerous creative and research projects. The organization's work has been shared with and loved by thousands of people around the world. PNSO collaborates with professional scientists and has been invited to many key laboratories around the world to create scientific works of art. Many works produced by PNSO staff members have been published in leading journals, including *Nature*, *Science*, and *Cell*. The organization has always been committed to supporting state-of-the-art scientific explorations. In addition, a large number of illustrations completed by PNSO staff members have been published and cited in hundreds of well-known media outlets, including the *New York Times*, the *Washington Post*, the *Guardian*, *Asahi Shimbun*, the *People's Daily*, BBC, CNN, Fox News, and CCTV. The works created by PNSO staff members have been used to help the public better understand the latest scientific discoveries and developments. In the public education sector, PNSO has held joint exhibitions with scientific organizations including the American Museum of Natural History and the Chinese Academy of Sciences. PNSO has also completed international cooperation projects with the World Young Earth Scientist Congress and the Earth Science Matters Foundation, thus helping young people in different parts of the world understand and appreciate scientific art.

KEY PROJECTS

I. Darwin: An Art Project of Life Sciences
*The models are all life-sized and are based on fossils found around the world
1.1 Dinosaur fossils
1.2 Pterosaurs fossils
1.3 Aquatic reptile fossils
1.4 Ancient mammals of the Cenozoic Era
1.5 Chengjiang biota: animals in the Early Cambrian from fossils discovered in Chengjiang, Yunnan, China
1.6 Jehol biota: animals in the Mesozoic Era from fossils discovered in Jehol, Western Liaoning, China
1.7 Early and extinct humans
1.8 Ancient animals that coexisted with early and extinct humans
1.9 Modern humans
1.10 Animals of the *Felidae* family
1.11 Animals of the *Canidae* family
1.12 Animals of the Proboscidea order

1.13 Animals of the *Ursidae* family

II. Galileo: An Art Project of Constellations
2.1 Classical Greek mythological characters that relate to the 88 modern constellations
2.2 Classical Greek mythological characters that relate to 10 constellation guardian deities

III. Starland Paradise: A Project Creating a Wonderful Science Literary World for Children
3.1 Science Literature for Children series: *Starland Paradise: Dingdong Bear and Twinkle Dino*
3.2 Education courses developed using Science Literature for Children series: *Starland Paradise: Dingdong Bear and Twinkle Dino*

IV. Haven: A Scientific Art Project about Our World
4.1 Guanguan: I have a T-rex, A Science Literary Project for Children
4.2 Guanguan: I have a Zoo, A Science Comic Project
4.3 The 12 Chinese Zodiac Animals, A Science Literary Project for Children

V. Laborer: Scientific Art Project to Express Humans' Production Activities
5.1 Common food crops
5.2 Common fruits
5.3 Common vegetables
5.4 Labor and Creation: Based on the Processes and Results of Humans' Production Activities

VI. Great Rivers: An Art Project on the History of Human Civilization
6.1 Great Thinkers in Human History from the Perspective of Scientific Art
6.2 Natural Landscape and Human Cultural Heritage: the Case of Mount Tai, China
6.3 Geographical Landscape and Life Phenomenon: the Case of Tanzania
6.4 Man-made Landscape and Natural Environment: the Case of Beijing